Free Woman

The Life and Times of Victoria Woodhull

Free Woman

The Life and Times of Victoria Woodhull

Marion Meade

OPEN ROAD

INTEGRATED MEDIA

NEW YORK

Copyright © 1976, 2011 by Marion Meade

ISBN 978-1-4976-3898-3

This edition published in 2014 by Open Road Integrated Media, Inc.
345 Hudson Street
New York, NY 10014
www.openroadmedia.com

Acknowledgments

For their help during my research for this book, I would like to thank the staffs of the Sophia Smith Collection at Smith College, the Schlesinger Library at Radcliffe College, and the New-York Historical Society.

For my daughter—Alison

Contents

Foreword

The Presidential election of 1920 was one of the most important in U.S. history. This ground-breaking event marked the first time that women were eligible to vote, and millions of them showed up at the polls. (Republican Warren G. Harding was elected.)

After a seven decades-long battle for the vote, who remembered, for instance, the historic election of 1872—won by the incumbent Ulysses S. Grant—an election noteworthy because another of the candidates that year was a woman. Not that people had taken Victoria Woodhull seriously at the time.

"I am too many years ahead of this age," observed Woodhull, and that is exactly right. As there was no place for her in the 19th century she was soon forgotten. But in the 1970s, when another generation of feminists was banding together to fight for their civil rights, her accomplishments seemed worth celebrating. Was the time ripe for a comeback, I wondered?

Victoria Claflin Woodhull was an intense, statuesque beauty, one of ten children born to a poor family in Homer, Ohio. After only a few years of schooling she married at fifteen and had two children with a husband who turned out to be an alcoholic.

And yet, astonishingly, just a dozen years later she and her sister Tennessee rolled into New York City and proceeded to make a name for themselves in the business world. With backing from the tycoon Cornelius Vanderbilt, the independent-minded sisters embarked on two unprecedented ventures: a Wall Street investment firm, and a muckraking newspaper (it once printed Marx and Engel's *Communist Manifesto*).

For years, feminists had struggled to win equal rights.

Along came Woodhull, aglow with confidence. What set the outsider apart from other activists was a combination of brains, beauty, and brass.

Doyennes of the women's rights movement initially turned up their noses at Woodhull. The power players at the time were Susan B. Anthony, a sober 50-year-old unmarried former teacher, and Elizabeth Cady Stanton, 55-year-old wife of an attorney and mother of seven. For years this conservative team, along with many other veteran feminists, had toiled over practical strategies to bring about change. The ambitious Woodhull pressed ahead without much regard for their hard work or their safe political methods. Confrontational, she had views of her own. In addition, she personally was not entirely respectable. Unlike most women she worked outside the home, and she was also divorced with a messy private life. Clearly she was a person they couldn't ignore, and so despite misgivings the suffragists determined to work with her.

She scooped the honor of being the first woman to address Congress. Before the House Judiciary Committee, she presented legal arguments to prove that the Constitution already gave women the right to vote. The 14th and 15th Amendments granted that right to all citizens. Were not women citizens?

If the feminist establishment had a problem with Woodhull's controversial political approach, the average American found utterly shocking her advanced views on sexual freedom (dubbed "free love" in the 19th century). In all matters, personal and political, she rejected the double standard. As a result, she was presumed to be a prostitute.

For a time, Woodhull was one of the most prominent women in the whole country. She kept making news:
first female stockbroker
first woman to publish her own weekly newspaper
first woman to address Congress
first woman to run for President, on the Equal Rights party ticket
After that it was downhill, though, because her fighting

spirit broke, little by little. Marrying a banker, she moved to England, where politics would play no part in her life. She lived to see American women get the vote, dying in 1927 at the age of 88.

A modest biography of Woodhull would, I hoped, bring her back to public view. For me, the book was a restoration project, as well as a labor of love.

In pre-computer days, biographers wrote on typewriters—mine was a trim little Olivetti Lettera 22—and we gathered our material by old-fashioned foot work. Without the Internet, we were obliged to trot from library to library, filling out call slips and making notes on 3 x 5 index cards. Much of my research was done at the New-York Historical Society, Columbia's Butler Library, and the Boston Public Library. Copies of *Woodhull and Claflin's Weekly* were available on microfilm at the New York Public Library. My odyssey took me to Vassar, Radcliffe, and Smith to consult their extensive files on the suffrage movement. I also managed to locate a rare 1928 biography with the repugnant title, *The Terrible Siren*, a deplorable portrayal of Woodhull as a trashy tabloid celebrity.

Free Woman was published by Alfred A. Knopf as a young adult biography in 1976. I would have earned more working at Burger King. The publisher paid an advance against royalties of $1,500 and invited me to a company book party at a Third Avenue ice cream parlor in Manhattan.

From time to time, I received inquiries about optioning the book for a "biopic," but enthusiasm never translated into a movie. Then, in 1980, a lavish musical about Woodhull opened on Broadway. "This show," wrote one critic, "looks like a dinner theater's homegrown answer to "Hello, Dolly!" and it's becalmed almost to a fault. You want a good night's sleep? Pay your money and rest in peace." Unsurprisingly, *Onward Victoria* closed after a single performance.

Several dozen countries have been governed by female presidents or prime ministers by now, some of the most famous women being Margaret Thatcher, Golda Meir, and Indira Gandhi. In the U.S., California congresswoman

Nancy Pelosi, former Speaker of the House of Representatives (2007-2011), was third in line for the office of President (after Vice President Joseph Biden).

And of course Hillary Rodham Clinton narrowly lost her bid for the Democratic nomination to Barack Obama.

No doubt, history is still catching up to Victoria Woodhull.

> Marion Meade
> January 2011
> New York City

$\mathscr{P}$reface

She was the first woman in American history to seek the Presidency; in most people's eyes that made her a monster. Among the mildest of the names they called her was "Mrs. Satan." In 1872 the notion of a woman President had sufficient power to shock most people. In an age when females were thought too ignorant to vote, it was a revolutionary idea.

Perhaps others before her may have shared the dream; if so, they never dared expose themselves to ridicule. Political ambition was considered, to say the least, unwomanly. For that matter, any kind of worldly ambition was thought to be unnatural for a woman.

After all, those who had given birth to our nation weren't called the Founding Fathers for nothing. Yes, America had been a brave new experiment in government. True, we were a democracy proclaiming liberty and justice for all. But the question of who shall lead and who shall follow had been decided at the outset. Indeed, it had never even been debated. Politics was deemed a suitable occupation only for men.

Where were the Founding Mothers? They were home raising their children, cooking, and keeping house. These functions are important, and they were even more vital to life in frontier days than now, but women lacked the freedom to choose other work. A woman with political ambitions kept them to herself. If she were extraordinarily lucky, she might marry a man who would someday win high office and then she could be a First Lady. To wish for more was madness and delusion.

No doubt Victoria Woodhull was a bit odd. Few ordinary

women would have possessed the emotional energy to pursue her impossible dream. How she first stumbled upon the idea is difficult to determine. When she spoke of her past, she was apt to make it sound like a soap opera. She claimed modestly that the Presidency wasn't her idea at all. A vision had appeared to her, a being in a Greek tunic who prophesied that one day she would lead her people. Perhaps so. But one fact remains: even a gutsy woman like Victoria Woodhull could not openly declare that she wanted to be President simply because she wanted to be President.

She rudely violated conventional ideas of what was proper behavior for her sex, and she rejected totally the traditional view that a woman has no right to be ambitious or competitive. Whether as presidential nominee, radical feminist, stockbroker, newspaper editor, socialist, public speaker, "free lover," or divorcee, Victoria Woodhull gloried in her independence.

She was a genuine rebel and nonconformist who possessed a mind of her own which she determined to use. Particularly remarkable was her confidence in her own ability; she believed in Victoria Woodhull. She coveted power, fully aware of the responsibility that goes with it, and when she aimed for the White House, it was not an empty gesture. She meant business.

Her ideas as much as her actions made nineteenth-century America exceedingly nervous. "I anticipate criticism," she once declared. A good thing, too, for she got it.

And yet, because she happened to be an extraordinarily beautiful woman and a compelling speaker, people were sufficiently disarmed to look, listen, and read about her.

She outraged her contemporaries. They may not have liked her. Bur they couldn't ignore her.

In the end, she failed. But at least she dared. She lived her revolutionary beliefs while struggling to live in a hostile world and battling to change it.

History books have omitted Victoria Woodhull. When her presidential campaign has been mentioned, it has rated a token line, usually written in jest. But lately her name is being heard once again. Feminist anthologies now include samples of her eloquent speeches. A documentary film, *Our North American Foremothers*, gives proper credit to her presidential aspirations. And, in New York City, a group of musicians recently formed the Victoria Woodhull Women's Marching Band.

It would be reassuring to conclude that if she had lived today, her quest for the Presidency might have succeeded. But such a conjecture would surely be misleading. The 1970s were only slightly more prepared than the 1870s were to accept a woman President.

The time for a Victoria Woodhull still lies somewhere over the horizon.

1
Those Crazy Claflins

If a girl could choose the kind of family in which to be born, she wouldn't pick the Claflins of Homer, Ohio. A loud, quarrelsome bunch, they were obsessed by status and money, probably because they had so little of either. They moved a lot, sometimes at the request of their neighbors, because the father, Buck Claflin, was not above pulling a shady business deal now and then. The fifth of his seven children (several more died in infancy), Vicky always regarded her relatives as her cross to bear.

Vicky was different from the rest of the Claflins. She was a winsomely beautiful child with cornflower blue eyes, silky brown curls, and a delicate profile. Her aristocratic bearing won her the nickname "Little Queen." Perhaps this was also due to the fact that Queen Victoria had been crowned ruler of England the year before Vicky's birth. More likely it reflected her unusual poise. She acted regal, like one born to command.

Sometimes she would round up several of the neighboring farmers' children and lecture to them. Standing atop an old Indian mound near her house, she would preach of what might befall them if they weren't good.

"Sinners, repent!" she'd exclaim, borrowing the juiciest phrases remembered from the religious revival meetings she attended with her mother. When the kids grew bored, Vicky would switch to a hair-raising tale of an Indian scalping. For a while the children would listen excitedly, but even so, she couldn't hold their attention for long. They didn't like her. Which was true of the way the adult citizens of Homer felt about all the Claflins.

Homer—where Victoria was born on September 23, 1838— hardly looked like a town at all. Slumbering among the rolling Ohio hills about forty miles northeast of Columbus, it existed mainly for the benefit of the surrounding farmers. There were a few homes, a store, a church, a post office, a log-cabin school, and a mill for grinding grain. Vicky's father owned the mill.

Like most rural villages, Homer was a quiet place inhabited by sober, respectable folk. Nothing very exciting happened there. The women cooked, sewed, and kept house. They raised their children to be well-behaved and say "yes, ma'am" and "thank you." The men tended their businesses and farms, shoed horses, split wood. Everyone went to church on Sunday.

As far as the villagers were concerned, the only good thing about the Claflins was that they lived on the edge of town. People said that Buck was shiftless and dishonest. Once, according to town gossip, he tried to spend some counterfeit money. When the sheriff came to arrest him, Buck pulled a $100 bill from his pocket and ate it.

The housewives of Homer clucked disapprovingly about the Claflin children, who always had tangled hair and smudged faces, wore filthy calico dresses, and generally ran wild. "Those young'uns aren't even properly fed," they declared because the Claflin youngsters were in the habit of showing up at their doors, asking for something to eat.

Buck's ramshackle house, badly needing a coat of paint, was considered an eyesore. Beds, invariably unmade, littered the porch and yard. Dirty, unkempt youngsters wandered in and out, while the house rattled with screams and fights. Roxanna Claflin was hardly a perfect housekeeper and mother. In fact, one of the loudest voices was hers. She had a violent temper.

Buck Claflin would not have gone along with modern notions of child rearing. He belonged to the spare-the-rod-

and-spoil-the-child school. He was neither a patient nor a particularly kind man. When his children displeased him, he beat them. A braided switch was kept handy for this very purpose Apparently it got a lot of use. As Vicky would recall many years later, her father "was impartial in his cruelty to all his children. I have no remembrance of a father's kisses."

In her own way, Roxanna was somewhat more loving. At times, she'd nag her youngsters unmercifully or box their ears. Then, full of remorse, she'd caress them and tearfully croon prayers, thanking God for such wonderful children.

Having such parents must have been upsetting for a sensitive, intensely serious child like Vicky. Sometimes she hated them, and yet she vaguely understood that they were barely staying afloat in a sea of economic worries.

The first Claflin to come to the New World was a paid soldier who left Scotland in 1661. Despite the family's early arrival on these shores, none of them managed to distinguish themselves in any way whatsoever. Buck had tried a dozen different trades and not one of them had worked out successfully. A tall man with a jutting chin, he'd lost the sight in one eye from a childhood accident, playing Indians with bows and arrows.

As a youth, he liked to hang out with gamblers and horse traders who congregated in the river towns of eastern Pennsylvania. Desperately anxious to be a successful wheeler and dealer himself, he occasionally had a lucky card game or business deal. For a while he kept store, then traded horses for a living. Finally, he got a job as stablekeeper for a rich family in the town of Selingsgrove, Pennsylvania.

There he met and married Roxanna Hummel, whose father owned the Rising Sun tavern. Although Roxanna couldn't read or write, she had a quick mind and strong religious convictions, both of which appealed to Buck.

Life wasn't easy for the young couple. As they pushed on from town to town, trying to eke out a living, the babies came at regular intervals. One winter they were left homeless when a blizzard destroyed their house.

In spite of their difficulties, maybe because of them, the

Claflins developed a very strong sense of family loyalty. They fought among themselves, but when criticized by outsiders, they defended one another fiercely. Mama Claflin was always standing up for her boisterous brood. Once, when they were sent home from Sunday school for acting bratty, she promptly trotted down to the church and gave the preacher a tongue-lashing.

Still, the quiet Vicky stood apart from her family. The only one she truly felt close to was her sister Tennessee, seven years younger. Humorous, spunky, and forthright, Tennie admired Vicky and followed her around like a worshipful puppy.

The days before the Civil War, when Vicky was a child, were an age of comparative innocence in American history. It was that period of primitive simplicity recalled so nostalgically by Mark Twain—a benign never-never land where boys like Huck Finn and Tom Sawyer could drift, carefree, down the Mississippi River on a raft. By contrast, life was altogether different for a girl. At least for a girl like Vicky.

In those days, few parents believed in educating girls. Vicky's were no exception. Roxanna Claflin had not gone to school, and as far as she could tell, learning to read and write was a sheer waste of time.

"But, Mama, I want to go to school," begged Vicky.

"Why?" Roxanna demanded in exasperation. "I reckon it'd be different if you was a boy. Ain't no use under God's sun for girls to have book learnin'. God made women for raisin' young 'uns and keepin' house."

Her determined daughter pestered and pestered. Finally, when Vicky was eight, Roxanna relented. Vicky began attending the one-room log schoolhouse in town. Some of the other children hated school, and when they acted up, the teacher punished them by putting wire clothespins on their noses.

Vicky, however, was a model student. She loved reciting her ABCs and doing sums on a jagged piece of slate. She had a quick mind, and the teacher paid a lot of attention to her.

Her classmates, less admiring, would tease, "Teacher's pet, teacher's pet." Vicky ignored them.

What troubled her most was that she didn't get to school very often. Yes, her mother had consented, but when housework had to be done, it was a different story.

"Victoria," her mother would announce sharply in the morning, "it's bread-bakin' day. You hear me!" That meant Vicky would stay home and bake bread. Another day, she would make soap and candles.

By this time, her oldest sister, Margaret Ann, was married and already had several small children. She, too, needed help. Roxanna generously offered Vicky's services. Vicky, of course, was not consulted. She had no choice but to trudge over to Margaret Ann's house where there was always something to do; Vicky made fires, washed and ironed, cut wood, spaded the vegetable garden, and took care of her sister's babies.

She resented it. She didn't even like her sister that much, and she certainly didn't appreciate being Margaret Ann's maid. Oh, why couldn't she go to school where she could imagine worlds of beauty and adventure far removed from her own bleak life in Homer?

For three years, Vicky went to school whenever she could. Then, one day, her education ended abruptly. So did living in Homer. Buck Claflin, always on the lookout for ways to make a fast dollar, had discovered a new idea called "fire insurance." By paying the insurance company a few cents a year, he would get back the full value of his gristmill should a fire occur.

Practically nobody in Homer had any property they thought worth insuring and when Buck insured his mill, the news soon traveled all over town. It became the chief topic of gossip. People gossiped even harder when Buck's mill happened to burn to the ground one Sunday night. In fact, they acted downright suspicious.

When Buck tried to collect his insurance, he learned it wouldn't be quite so easy as he'd imagined. There were questions, lots of them. People in Homer hadn't the slightest doubt that Buck had set the fire himself. They said he'd always been a crook. "He should be tarred and feathered!" they cried.

Faced with a major scandal, Buck quietly dropped his insurance claim and slipped out of town. Homer was delighted to see him go. Unfortunately, there was one small problem. He'd left his family behind. Did that mean he would be returning? Not if the citizens of Homer had anything to say about it.

Some of the more practical folks hit upon a perfect solution. They decided to hold a benefit bazaar and raise money to send this poor abandoned family to join its scalawag husband and father. What could be more charitable? And what easier way to get rid of undesirables?

Afterward, the people of Homer had no regrets. They discovered that Buck, who had run the post office in his spare time, thoroughly deserved his bad reputation. The man who took his place as postmaster found a trunk full of letters, each one stating that money was being enclosed. All the envelopes were empty.

At the age of eleven, it isn't pleasant to be uprooted from your home and practically escorted out of town in disgrace. Nor is it easy to know you're not wanted. For several years the Claflin tribe roamed around Ohio, stopping at one town and then another. How long would they stay? Vicky never knew. It depended on whether Buck thought there was an opportunity to make money. Sometimes he'd go into partnership with other men, but the businesses never lasted long. And, once again, the Claflins would move on.

Finally, traveling almost full circle, they came to a halt in Mount Gilead, a small town not far from Homer. It wasn't because Mount Gilead offered such lush pickings for Buck's business schemes. Rather, it was because Margaret Ann and her husband had recently settled there.

On the surface, the humiliations of such a chaotic existence appeared to wash over Vicky. She remained as she'd always been—solemn and soft-spoken. All the hurts became unimportant because she had a secret. Once, when she'd been younger, she had seen a vision. A beautiful young man in a dazzling white Grecian tunic had appeared to her. He looked like an angel.

"You will know wealth and fame one day," he promised gently. "You will live in a mansion, in a city surrounded by ships, and you will become ruler of your people."

That, Vicky later insisted, was how she first got the idea she might be an important person someday. Far from disbelieving the incredible prophecy, the enthralled little girl thought it sounded quite reasonable. Hadn't she always felt special, like she didn't belong to the Claflins? This proved it.

When she told her parents of the vision, they saw nothing extraordinary about it and soon forgot. Not Vicky. She felt sure that a special destiny awaited her. Somewhere. Someday.

Actually, the Claflins paid no attention to her miraculous vision because Vicky was always seeing things. From the age of three, she showed signs of being clairvoyant. She had the rare ability of being aware of distant objects or events which could not be known through ordinary sight, hearing, taste, or touch. Sometimes she would scare other children by reading their minds or telling them where lost objects could be found. She could also describe events before they happened.

Most of us have a small amount of this intuitive talent— we call it having a "premonition" or a "hunch." A few people, like psychic Jeanne Dixon who warned of President Kennedy's assassination before it occurred, seem to have highly developed powers of intuition. Both Vicky and her sister Tennie had this extra sense of perception.

The late 1840s was a period in American history that abounded with new ideas. People eagerly sought ways to perfect their own lives or to improve the world. Some thought vegetarianism or eating health foods was the answer. Others crusaded against alcohol. The Abolitionists insisted that America would be Utopia if the slaves were freed.

And in Seneca Falls, New York, a small group of women had embarked upon a passionate struggle for equal rights.

In 1848, Elizabeth Cady Stanton and Lucretia Mott had organized the first Women's Rights Convention. They were determined to change the conditions that had made women into second-class citizens, indeed had denied them the right to behave as full human beings. For their trouble, the feminists who congregated at Seneca Falls were bombarded with ridicule.

The Reign of Petticoats, scoffed one newspaper headline. *Blasphemy!* squealed another.

But twelve-year-old Vicky, in the backwoods of Ohio, knew nothing of these events. Nor were her parents the kind of people who might be attracted to new intellectual ideas; their interests revolved solely around making money. That's why it is not surprising that one new idea did catch their attention.

At that time, there was enormous interest in the occult. Serious, educated people discussed reincarnation; tried to communicate with the dead through mediums; and patronized psychics who could tune in to their past, present, and future. Two of the most famous psychics were Kate and Margaret Fox, a pair of New York sisters who were collecting bushels of publicity and money from their seances. So widespread were reports of the Fox sisters' feats that their success even reached Mount Gilead and the notice of Buck Claflin.

Two sisters who told fortunes? Two sisters who were said to be making a fortune? Buck suddenly realized that he was sitting on a gold mine. Didn't he have two daughters who were clairvoyant?

Before Vicky and Tennie knew what was happening, he'd installed them in the parlor of a Mount Gilead boardinghouse where they soon were busily reading people's futures. Although the Claflin sisters received a good deal of attention, Vicky did not feel entirely comfortable. She took her gifts of prophecy quite seriously. Also, she couldn't turn on her power of insight whenever she pleased. It doesn't work that way, she protested.

In that case, Buck advised his daughters, they should fake it.

And so Vicky and Tennie shrugged and did their best to give the customers their money's worth.

After a while, it wasn't much fun at all. When they weren't telling fortunes, there were the endless chores and the petty quarreling at home. Vicky longed to wear pretty clothes, to dance and have a good time. Secretly, she dreamed of getting away from the rowdy Claflins, of escaping from a tacky little town like Mount Gilead. Where was her Prince Charming, a beautiful young man who would swoop down and carry her off to his castle in the clouds? But she kept such thoughts to herself.

Now she was fourteen and had developed into a young woman. Not surprisingly, the boys in town began to notice her. It wasn't her blue eyes and delicate features, but her royal manner which made her stand out from the rest of the girls. She acted like a "lady." But Vicky wasn't interested in any oafish farm boy. None of them fitted her fantasies, nor the prophecy of wealth and fame.

One June morning, she was walking down the main street of Mount Gilead humming a little tune. There had been rain the night before, and the fragrant air smelled faintly of lilacs. Outside the post office, a man smiled at her She had never seen him before, but he was so handsome she couldn't help smiling back.

"Halloo," he said.

Vicky noticed that a lock of ebony silk hung down over his milky-white forehead. He had thick, sooty lashes and beautiful square teeth. His only defect, she thought, was a nervous twitch of the jaw.

"How do you do?" she murmured shyly.

Soon they were chatting like old friends. His name, he told her, was Canning Woodhull, and he had just arrived in town.

Obviously this fellow was no ordinary country boy. Tall and sophisticated, with charming manners and impeccable speech, he knew how to talk to a girl. Vicky could tell that he was older than she, as it turned out fourteen years her senior. As they spoke, she found out that he came from

Rochester, New York. He'd studied medicine in the East and now had come to Mount Gilead to set up a medical practice. A doctor! A gentleman! She couldn't help feeling awed.

"My little chick," he said gaily, "I want you to go with me to the Fourth of July picnic."

No one had ever called her "a little chick" before. She was filled with ecstasy.

Wide-eyed, she hurried home to ask her mother. Roxanna had no objections, but she quickly pointed out that Vicky had nothing to wear for so grand a date. It was true. Perhaps a dress could be borrowed, but the biggest problem was shoes. Hers were falling apart. They would never do, and there was no money to buy a new pair.

"I'll earn the money," exclaimed Vicky. "I'll pick apples and sell them and buy myself new shoes." And she did exactly that.

Apparently Vicky and Canning hit it off immediately. What happened during the Fourth of July celebration she never revealed. But on their way home that evening, Canning wasted no time in proposing.

"My little puss," he whispered tenderly, "tell your mother and father I want you for my wife."

It was like a fairy tale; in fact, it sounded too good to be true. The levelheaded Vicky must have told herself that, in real life, things don't happen so quickly. They hardly knew each other. How could Canning be sure that he really wanted to marry her?

These doubts didn't trouble her parents.

"A grand match!" bellowed Buck when he heard that his daughter had attracted a young man from a well-to-do Rochester family. Roxanna agreed.

Still, Vicky hesitated. After all, she was only fourteen and had never had a beau before. But her parents refused to listen.

"Marry him and the sooner the better," insisted Buck. "He might change his mind."

This made her very angry. Down deep, she felt hurt that her parents were so anxious to marry her off to the first man who came along. It didn't matter whether he was an eligible bachelor. They acted as if she were a piece of property, ready to be sold at the first decent offer. As far as her father was concerned, she murmured to herself, this was just another business deal, one too good to pass up.

At the same time, she knew that Canning Woodhull might be the answer to her prayers. He offered a perfect escape hatch from her humiliating life as one of the crazy Claflins. Marrying him would mean a new life—no more household drudgery, no more explosive scenes with her parents, no more fortune-telling, no more being poor and wearing tattered clothes. The prospect was very tempting.

Why shouldn't she marry this nice man who obviously adored her? As the wife of a doctor, wouldn't she have a house of her own and servants to do the work? Wouldn't she be a wealthy lady then?

Of course she would.

Two months later, a few weeks before her fifteenth birthday, she married Canning Woodhull.

2

From Frying Pan to Fire

During the early weeks of her marriage, Vicky discovered several startling facts about her new husband. To her dismay, the gentlemanly Canning much preferred drinking to practicing medicine. For that matter, he preferred drinking to any other activity.

It was scarcely a secret that Canning drank because she often smelled alcohol on his breath. But then, she reminded herself, what man didn't drink? In the nineteenth century, gathering in saloons and drinking was the most popular male pastime. It almost amounted to a national recreation. After work, or in the evenings, men would retire to the town saloon for a night of hearty boozing. Sometimes they left behind a considerable portion of their weekly wages.

Canning, however, showed no sign whatsoever of wanting to work. It was not unusual for him to start the day by taking a nip immediately upon arising from bed. By nightfall, pleasantly pickled, he seemed to forget that he now had a wife. For Canning, alcohol was certainly not a sport. It was a deep need, a habit, an addiction. In her naïveté, Vicky had married a genuine alcoholic.

Shortly after their wedding, she received another shock. One night Canning failed to come home. Sitting up until nearly dawn in their rented rooms, Vicky waited fearfully. What could be keeping him away? She imagined the worst. Surely he'd had an accident, perhaps he was lying dead somewhere. Finally, exhausted, she dozed off.

The next morning her husband reappeared, his eyes bloodshot but otherwise in fine spirits.

The anger rising in her voice, she demanded to know where he had been.

Apparently Canning did not have either the physical strength or the presence of mind to concoct an excuse. Looking sheepish, he blurted out the truth: he had spent the night with another woman.

The stunned girl could think of nothing to reply. Her tongue felt paralyzed, her mind numb. But she got the message. For an instant, she wished she were back home again, in the midst of the brawling Claflins where life may not have been ideal but at least there were no staggering miseries like those she felt right now.

"In a single day, I grew ten years older," she would recall many years later. "The shock awoke all my womanhood."

It also awoke her missionary zeal. "Sinners, repent," she had once sternly lectured the children in Homer. She had been play acting then; now she faced a real and terrible situation. She would reform Canning, she would save him.

The problem was, Canning did not want to be saved. When sober, he was a gentle, scholarly person, a man who adored children. At those times, Vicky loved him; but when he drank, she couldn't help despising him. Still, she was determined to be a good wife.

Although the new bride didn't admit it to anyone, she soon discovered that housekeeping bored her. More than that, she loathed washing and dusting, much preferring to sit at the window and dream about her destiny, which now seemed like a bizarre joke. Bur if the floors were unscrubbed and the bread unbaked, Canning never noticed.

She began to feel that marriage was horribly depressing. One day she suddenly had an inspiration. She suggested to Canning that they visit his family in Rochester. Surely they would want to meet his wife.

That being one of Canning's sober moments, he immediately agreed. In fact, he wondered why he hadn't thought of the idea himself.

Vicky wisely refrained from mentioning her real motive. Once back with his very proper family, she hoped that Canning would stop drinking and begin to think about medicine. So far, they had lived on a small allowance from his father, but most of the money went for whiskey. Obviously they couldn't continue that way indefinitely.

As the time for their departure neared, Vicky began to feel nervous. What if the fancy Woodhulls didn't like her? What if they snubbed her because she wasn't a lady?

Unfortunately, her fears turned out to be justified. Canning's father, Judge Woodhull, treated her cordially enough. But her elegant mother-in-law and the other women in the family were outraged by her ignorance and what they considered her lower-class vulgarity. They didn't bother to hide their scorn. Cruelly, they laughed at her manners, her poor grammar, her small-town clothes, her lack of education.

Once, Vicky's stomach turned over when she overheard Mrs. Woodhull say bitterly to a visitor, "How could my son have married a trashy little baggage like her!" Feverish with humiliation, Vicky ran to her room.

"The old cat!" she cried. From behind her locked door came the sound of terrible smothered sobbing.

Eventually she managed to bury this painful experience. But the grudge she felt against so-called respectable people, her social superiors, would explode into violent rebellion twenty years later when she fought against the hypocrisy of the upper classes.

In all respects, the trip could be counted a fiasco. Back in Mount Gilead, Canning resumed his drinking and womanizing. Once again, the desperate Vicky thought a change of environment might solve his problem. Moving was a solution she unconsciously had picked up from her childhood: if anything goes wrong, get out of town. She and her husband, following the old pattern of the Claflins, began moving from one place to another.

First they went to Chicago where Canning rented a one-story frame house. Now almost sixteen, Vicky felt happy because she was expecting a baby. Maybe fatherhood would make Canning realize he must work. At least she hoped so.

That winter was one of the coldest in Chicago's history. The thermometer seemed stuck below zero, and because Canning rarely remembered to buy firewood, there was often no heat in the house. On some mornings, Vicky awoke to find icicles on the bedpost.

As the time for the birth drew near, she began to panic. Where would they find the money for a doctor when her labor began? But Canning was all sweet talk and promises. Telling her not to worry, he reminded her that he was a doctor.

Vicky felt uneasy, but she had to trust him. There was no one else.

It was a long, difficult birth. True to his word, Canning stayed with her, but he was half drunk. As the agonizing hours passed, he became even shakier. Finally it was over. She had given birth to a boy.

Vicky heard Canning moving toward the door. Although she begged him not to leave her, Canning mumbled that he was just going for a walk. He would be back soon.

As the door slammed, the exhausted Vicky, too weak to weep, fell asleep. Later that evening, Canning returned to care for her and the infant. But three weeks later he disappeared.

After a few days, when the larder was empty, Vicky left her baby, Byron, with a neighbor and set out to find her husband. She had not been out of the house since before Byron was born. Most of the time, they huddled under blankets to keep warm. Now, dressing, she could find no underwear or stockings or shoes. She had to make do with a calico dress and a pair of rubber boots for her feet.

Her first and most logical stop was the corner saloon, one of Canning's favorite hangouts. "Have you seen Dr. Woodhull?" she asked the owner.

"No, ma'am."

A man drinking ale at the bar spoke up. "Why, he's living

at Mrs. Petty's boardinghouse with his girl friend," the obliging customer volunteered.

A deadly rage began to seethe in Vicky. Shivering, she skidded along the glassy streets until she reached the house. Bursting in the front door, she found the boarders, Canning and his woman friend included, assembled around the table eating dinner. The sight of a big side of roast beef and a platter of fried potatoes made her feel nauseated.

When Canning looked up and saw her, he tried to explain and calm his furious wife. But Vicky refused to listen. Withering him with a single glance, she accused him of not loving her. "Your wife and child are starving while you sit here with your mistress, feeding your fat belly!"

That was only the beginning. Turning to the other startled diners, their forks suspended in mid-air, she proceeded to describe vividly what kind of man Dr. Woodhull really was. Her performance was as dramatic, and as vulgar, as any scene Roxanna Claflin had ever thrown. It was Vicky's first speech, and one of her most effective. Mrs. Petty's guests responded by angrily throwing Canning into the street.

And so her husband returned home, which was what she wanted. But nothing else changed. Gradually, however, a transformation began to take place in Vicky. She spent hour after hour brooding about her life. Like all young women in those days, she had grown up expecting to marry and be taken care of by her husband. Even a rascal like Buck always managed to provide a roof and food for his family. He knew his duty as a father and husband.

Canning was another story. He may have been aware of his duty, but he remained incapable of doing it. The truth was simple and unavoidable: Canning was sick. While she felt pity for him, Vicky slowly began to understand that she could not depend on him. Maybe she could never depend on any man.

In the future she would take care of herself, her baby, and yes, even Canning. If he would not be the head of their family, as tradition demanded, then the position went to her by default. From now on, she would give the orders.

Thinking led to action. The next thing Canning knew, they were on a boat bound for San Francisco. Once again, Vicky was trying the Claflin's last resort. Moving.

She had never seen a town like San Francisco. It was new. And wild. Five years earlier, in 1849, gold had been discovered in California. People had plenty of money. On the hillsides above the bay, makeshift wooden buildings went up overnight; down in the harbor, ships crowded the wharves. Didn't the man in her vision predict that she would live in a city of many ships, a city where she would rule over her people? Perhaps this is the place, she thought excitedly.

Leaving Canning and the baby at their hotel, hoping that her husband would stay away from the numerous saloons and gambling houses, Vicky set off to look for work. Her youth and prettiness swiftly won her a job selling cigars in a saloon. But the rough, bearded miners, full of leers and coarse remarks, made tears come to her eyes. She lacked the knack of answering their jokes in kind and, as a result, she sold few cigars. After a few days, the proprietor suggested that she find a more suitable line of work.

Money! In this city of riches, everybody seemed to have it but her. In those days, very few women had moneymaking skills. Most mothers routinely taught their daughters to sew, however, and that was the only skill Vicky could offer. She began traveling from house to house, asking if a dressmaker was needed.

One of her customers was Anna Cogswell, a popular actress who headed her own repertory company. Feeling sorry for the young woman, Anna suggested that she join the company as an actress. Before long, Vicky was playing minor parts and walk-ons.

Suddenly life seemed more wonderful than she had ever thought possible. She had an exciting new career. The actors and actresses impressed her as being tremendously glamorous and sophisticated. Some of it rubbed off on Vicky. Not only did she mature into a strikingly beautiful woman, but she also acquired poise, elegant manners, and a sense of style. Her speech improved greatly.

At home, life wasn't bad either. Canning's bouts with the bottle lessened, and he was proving to be a devoted father to Byron. Vicky had always had strength. Now the vitality she possessed as a child started to flow again.

One evening she was on stage in a drama called *The Corsican Brothers*. Dressed in a salmon gown trimmed with lace, she was waltzing in the ballroom scene when, above the music, she heard the voice of her sister Tennie.

"Victoria, come home," Tennie's voice called. And then, as clear as could be, a picture flashed before her eyes. Her mother and sister seemed to be stretching out their arms and crying, "Vicky, come home!"

Completely forgetting where she was, Vicky rushed off the stage. Still wearing her costume and makeup, she raced through the dark, misty streets back to her lodgings and told Canning to start packing. They were going home.

Despite her ominous vision, no disaster had befallen the Claflins. But they were delighted to have Vicky back again.

Buck hadn't changed a bit. Still the conniver, always searching for get-rich-quick schemes, he had now devised a new and profitable family business. He had decided to expand Tennie's psychic powers. If she could tell people their futures, she could also heal their illnesses. Accordingly, he organized a traveling medicine show which toured from town to town in a covered wagon with a ball-fringed top.

Everybody got into the act. Roxanna and Vicky's little sister Utica brewed salves and potions; brother Hebern distributed leaflets and brought in the customers; Buck acted as public relations man and general medical adviser. Tennie, the star of the show, was billed as "the Wonder Child who can cure the most obstinate diseases, including cancer, and in the course of a trance travel to any part of the world, and establish communication between the living and the dead." Her pretty childish face appeared on bottles of Roxanna's homemade medicine, *Miss Tennessee's Magnetic Elixir for Beautifying the Complexion and Cleansing the Blood*.

Years later, Vicky would tell a newspaper reporter, "I believe Tennie ought to use the gift God has given her but not in the mercenary way she was forced to use it. She had no right to prostitute her powers." She might just as well have been talking about herself because, for the next dozen years, she would use her psychic ability to earn a living. While she never resorted to the outright deception practiced by Tennie and the rest of the Claflins, there is no doubt she stretched her talent to please the customers.

The Claflins held a family conference at which Buck urged Vicky to join the medicine show.

"No, Pa," she refused. "I think it would be best if I struck out on my own."

Believing that she would do best in a large city, she chose Indianapolis. She decided to call herself a medium, one who specializes in treating patients and curing diseases.

Today psychic research is being done at a number of universities. All that has been determined is that some people do have the faculty of extrasensory perception. Some people are able to do healing. Some people possess knowledge that they have made no effort to acquire. But that is all that has been established. In the 1850s, nothing of the kind had been established. Still, there was a considerable market for the services that psychics had to offer.

With Canning and Byron, Vicky took rooms in the Bates House hotel and placed advertisements in Indianapolis newspapers. *Mrs. Victoria Claflin Woodhull, Spiritual Healer,* the announcements read. Her first customers were astounded to discover that Vicky could tell them their names, addresses, and the nature of their illnesses. In a few days, the news spread. The amazing Mrs. Woodhull became the talk of the town.

Vicky predicted future events, gave business advice, solved bank robberies, straightened the feet of the lame, and made the deaf hear again. Or so she later would claim. Apparently enough of her cures and predictions worked because the customers kept coming in and so did the money.

Along with prosperity, however, came tragedy. One morning Byron fell from a second-story window in the hotel. He was so badly injured that the doctors did not expect him to live. Eventually he recovered, but his brain was permanently damaged. For the rest of his life, he was severely retarded, physically and mentally.

Byron's accident plunged Vicky into the deepest depression. It seemed that every time she reached the brink of happiness and success, something terrible happened. Outwardly, her feelings didn't show. She continued to work, but money now meant little to her. Much of it she sent to her parents.

Inside, she felt wretched. Canning, as distraught over Byron as she was, had fewer and fewer sober periods. Once, in a drunken rage, he kicked her. As the months crept by, she began to long for more children. Sometimes, when she hugged and kissed Byron, he'd push her away because he didn't even know her.

"Dear God," she would pray, "please give me another child. A daughter who will be born with a beautiful body and a sound mind."

In April 1861 her daughter, Zulu Maud, was born, healthy and beautiful, just as Vicky had wished. For some inexplicable reason, Vicky allowed Canning to deliver the child. This time, he did more poorly than with Byron, ineptly cutting the umbilical cord too close to the skin and tying it so loosely that the string fell off. Afterward, he disappeared.

Several days later, Vicky was sitting up in bed near the window and saw Canning stumbling up the street. He started to climb the steps of the house across the street, mistaking it for his own.

When she saw her husband unable to find his way home, Vicky choked in despair. Then a horrible, comic thought occurred to her. "Now I have three children to look after."

The month Zulu Maud was born, life changed for most Americans. The explosive issue of slavery, which had slowly been tearing the country apart, now ignited the Civil War.

Enthusiastic young men rode off to join the army, promising their anxious mothers and sweethearts they would be home in a few weeks. Nobody returned in a few weeks. For many, the end came at places nobody had ever heard of—sites like Gettysburg and Appomattox. For the rest, it would be four years before the war ended and they rejoined their families.

The war had little effect on Vicky, or for that matter, on any of the Claflins. No fighting occurred in the Middle West. None of the Claflins enlisted in the army, and they had no opinions about slavery one way or the other. Politics, civil rights, and national affairs did not interest them. As far as they were concerned, this was somebody else's war.

In only one respect did the Civil War touch the Claflins. As is typical in wartime, people were restless and full of uncertainty; they also had money to spend. Both, figured Buck, couldn't hurt the spiritual-healing business. Vicky spent the war years traveling with her family. While Tennie was still the main attraction, Buck advertised himself as Dr. R. B. Claflin, American King of Cancers. He promised to cure anybody who followed his instructions. Telling fortunes was harmless enough, but with his cancer cures, Buck finally went too far.

In 1863 he opened a "cancer infirmary" at Ottawa, Illinois. When one of the patients died, Tennie was indicted for manslaughter. Before she could be jailed, the Claflins hurriedly stole out of town. After that, Buck decided that Tennie should retire from medicine and stick to a safe profession like fortune-telling.

In Cincinnati, and later Chicago, the family rented a house and put a sign in the front window: Tennessee Claflin and Victoria Woodhull, Clairvoyants. It was all very respectable, for the Claflins anyway, but troubles continued to hound them. Wherever they lived, the neighbors complained. Of course, the Claflins had never been a quiet family. Now there was a new complaint. Strange men were said to be entering the Claflin house after dark. Charges that the sisters must be operating a brothel were filed with the police.

While most of the men came to have their futures told, undoubtedly others were beaus of Tennie's. The neighbors' complaints amounted to nothing serious, but they did make life unpleasant for Vicky. She began to grow bitter. When she wasn't playing second fiddle to Tennie, the "Wonder Child" who was nearly twenty now, she was nursing Canning and caring for Byron and Zulu Maud. Ever since her daughter's birth, Vicky had been saying to herself, "What do I need Canning for? Why should I live with this man any longer?"

She had always believed that a wife should stay with her husband. For eleven years, she had been faithful to him. But theirs had never been a normal marriage. In those days, divorce was a disgrace and a scandal. Couples rarely divorced. But, as usual, the Claflins couldn't be bothered with what "nice people" did. Both of Vicky's older sisters, Margaret Ann and Polly, had divorced. Even impetuous Tennie, who had recently married a playboy named John Bartels, didn't remain with him long.

Vicky was certainly influenced by her sisters. She began to feel that marriage, especially a bad marriage, needn't be a life sentence. In 1864, she filed for divorce.

Separation from Canning brought no great improvement in her life, nor did it alter her mood which was decidedly bored. The gray months, and then years, passed slowly. She drifted along with the Claflins on their trips across Missouri, Arkansas, and Illinois, put up with their quarreling and their disorderly mode of existence. She knew that her life had gone awry.

In the past, one thought had comforted her—the vision that promised her fame, wealth, and power. She had believed in it. Now the dream began to fade. The years had flown by. She was old—twenty-eight—and all she had to show for those years was disappointment and unhappiness. Her memories were of neighbors who hated her, little boys who jeered at her on the street, visits from the police, moving to another town because she was unwanted. "Life," she thought, "has passed me by."

The next year found the Claflin clan in St. Louis. One spring day, when it was Vicky's turn to sit in the darkened parlor waiting for customers, a man entered to have his fortune told. He was good-looking, with chestnut brown hair and sideburns. He walked like a soldier. Before he could speak, Vicky felt herself going into a trance. She heard herself speaking astonishing words to the strange man.

"I see our futures linked," she calmly declared. "Our destinies will be bound together by the ties of marriage."

The man gazed at her serenely, as if her words were not the least surprising. His eyes were twinkling, though.

Colonel James Blood, a veteran of the Civil War, was now the city auditor of St. Louis, a man of importance in the community. He was also an intellectual radical.

What's more, he was already married.

No matter. Vicky's prediction proved right on target. Their destinies would be entwined for the next decade. Vicky desperately needed someone to push her in the right direction. Colonel Blood was that someone.

3

In Search of Her Destiny

The horses kicked up a yellow dust as the covered wagon rolled lazily along the backwoods road. Puffs of fleecy white clouds slid softly over a sky of baby blue. It was a peaceful afternoon in May 1866, not the kind of day for the crazy adventure upon which Vicky and James had embarked.

From the moment they had met, they had been powerfully drawn to each other. Perhaps it had been Vicky's first words to James, "I see our futures linked." Neither of them could explain it, but, to their mutual amazement, James abruptly cut all ties and walked away from his life as if it had never existed. He suggested they go away together. Others, Mrs. Blood to name one, would describe it in blunter terms and call it "running away." But James and Vicky, oblivious to everyone else, were in love.

Behind them lay the great Mississippi River and the city of St. Louis. Left behind, too, were the Claflins and Vicky's children and James's wife and daughter, not to mention his position as city auditor.

Ahead of them stretched the summer. Their wagon rambled westward through emerald orchards and olive-green farmlands, from one tiny village to another, hamlets that reminded Vicky of Homer and Mount Gilead. When they needed food and money, they stopped. James would stroll about the main street telling the curious villagers about the clairvoyant "Madame Victoria" who could look into their pasts and futures. As the townspeople lined up to have their fortunes told, James collected their money.

For a change, Vicky didn't care about money. She felt in a gay holiday mood. All her fire and joy, buried for so many years under the weight of a disastrous marriage and a handicapped child, bubbled to the surface. At last she felt free.

In the weeks that followed, Vicky and James spent all their hours together. They became lovers. And they talked. It is not surprising that the subjects they first discussed were marriage, love, and sex. Both had been unhappily wed, both had felt imprisoned by their marriages.

"Why can't people be free?" cried Vicky. "Married people think they own each other. Why can't people love whom they like, even if they do happen to be married?"

"Women as well as men," James added.

"Of course," declared Vicky. "What is right for one sex is right for the other."

But she knew from her own experience that women couldn't do as they pleased. Didn't she allow her father to practically sell her into marriage? Didn't she remain true to Canning even after all love for him had fled? In reality, men had freedom; women did not.

"Women know nothing but blind obedience to their fathers and husbands," she told James. "They do whatever their menfolk say."

She thought of the countless women who had come to have their fortunes told. Over and over, she heard the same stories. After a while, it began to sound like all of female America had only one story. Women had no opportunities.

Their education was scant or nonexistent. They could not earn their own livings, except at the most menial jobs. Everything depended on finding a man to marry. Then, cooped and caged, they had to do whatever the men wished them to.

And the troubles women had with men! Vicky had listened to them all. There were the desperate unmarried girls who had no future, no chance to express sexual feelings, until they found a husband. Married women, locked into loveless marriages, were not much better off. It was a wife's duty to sleep with her husband whenever he demanded sex.

If there was one thing Victorian America felt sure about, it was that normal women didn't experience sexual desire. Men, of course, did. But normal women had relations with their husbands only for the sake of having children.

No, decided Vicky, women had no control over their lives, much less their bodies.

"Marriage is the most damnable outrage upon women that was ever conceived," she suddenly burst out. "Someday we will rebel."

To her surprise, James did not disagree. In fact, he confided to her that he believed in "free love." Vicky had heard of it. Of all the idealistic doctrines invented during the nineteenth century, "free love" was the one which made most people turn pale with horror. They mistakenly equated it with immorality and promiscuity.

Actually, the "free lovers" thought highly of love and sex—so highly that they believed sex should take place only between two persons who felt genuine affection for each other. They said it was dishonest for a man and a woman, even if married, to make love if they felt no love. The "free lovers" also believed that sex should be as free and natural as eating or sleeping.

Such ideas scandalized almost everyone. The years during which Vicky lived—called the Victorian era after England's Queen Victoria—were probably the most prudish in history. Supposedly, a girl could not be alone with a boy; they had to be accompanied by a chaperone. From the earliest age, all signs of sexuality were stamped out of girls. They were not to sit with their legs crossed or to sleep on soft beds. Their bodies were encased in stiff corsets. Stimulants such as tea, coffee, or alcohol were forbidden.

Anything concerning the body was unmentionable. That included the way people talked. "Leg" was a naughty word; instead, a leg was called a "limb." The word "breast" was also forbidden—people spoke of "the bosom of a chicken."

Not only was speech censored but art as well. A man

named Thomas Bowdler went through the works of Shakespeare and hacked out everything "which cannot with propriety be read aloud in the family." Another man, Noah Webster, wrote a new version of the Bible because he thought the original too risqué.

In every period of repression, a few people rebel. Most of them complain bitterly but continue to lead more or less conventional lives. Others—the militant rebels—speak out to call a lie a lie. They also defy the conventions in their own lives by practicing what they believe.

Without being aware of it, Vicky was one of these militants. So was James Blood. In every way, he could be called a radical, an extremist. Not only did he believe in "free love," but he also told Vicky about other new ideas that had never penetrated her limited world.

For example, he spoke of new political systems such as socialism, which sounded fairer than the capitalistic American system. "It's wrong," he said, "when a few people have plenty of money and the rest have to scramble for enough to eat." James described an ideal society in which there would be no prejudice or hypocrisy, in which people would not be blinded by fear and jealousy, where people— women and men—would lead truly free lives.

To her amazement, Vicky learned that a few women had already begun to revolt. They called themselves "feminists," which simply means that they strongly believed women should enjoy the same rights and privileges as men. Eventually they would be called by other names: women's righters, suffragists (because they sought the right to vote), even the cute label "suffragettes."

James told her about Elizabeth Cady Stanton and Lucretia Mott, who had rewritten the Declaration of Independence. Other women, following the example of Amelia Bloomer, had abandoned petticoats in favor of loose trousers gathered at the ankles. And when another prominent feminist, Lucy Stone, had married, she defied tradition by deciding to keep her own name. Her husband, Henry Blackwell, heartily approved.

Whether it was history, feminism, philosophy, or

economics, everything they discussed made sense to Vicky. She could relate all of it to her own experiences. Since childhood, she had hidden many of her inner thoughts and feelings. Secretly she had suspected that she might be a little mad. Now she realized that she was not mad and she was not alone.

Never before had she known a man like James. Gentle, courteous, and kind, he spoke to her as an equal, not as a grown-up child who could not comprehend because she was a woman. And comprehend she did. Everything he told her, she immediately understood. What's more, she invariably added some original view of her own. James was amazed to learn that she had practically no formal education. He thought she was the most intelligent woman he had ever met.

At last, Vicky summoned the nerve to tell him of her childhood vision, the prophecy that she would become a leader. He didn't laugh or even smile. He listened seriously. "Why not?" he replied. "Doesn't a woman sit on the throne of England? Why shouldn't a woman be President of the United States?"

Spring became summer. May, June, and July passed. Vicky and James realized their vagabond life could not last forever. They must go home and put their lives in order.

Shortly after their return to St. Louis, James divorced his wife. While he and Vicky had been roving the countryside, the idea of living together without being married had seemed like a wonderful, liberating notion. Now they were having second thoughts. For one thing, Roxanna Claflin took an instant dislike to James. Perhaps she was put off by his education and manners, but more likely she was jealous of the influence he had on Vicky. Roxanna, no less puritanical than the rest of the country, was outraged that James did not plan to make "an honest woman" of her daughter.

Actually, Vicky might have ignored her mother's feelings but for one fact. Roxanna's reaction was similar to everyone else's. Perhaps Vicky looked ahead to a time when she would be seeking a position of leadership. Who would accept a woman who lived with a man without being married? Her background was not terribly respectable anyway. Why deliberately add another offensive mark to her record?

What she did would not be much better in the eyes of the public. But it satisfied both Vicky's and James's conviction that marriage must be open and free. They married and the following year filed secretly for divorce. Thus they satisfied the legal and moral codes as well as their own desires for a relationship that would rest only on love, freely given.

Remembering Lucy Stone, who declined to take her husband's name, Vicky also decided to keep the name Woodhull. This decision, incidentally, confused people later on and gave them one more reason to turn against her. They assumed that she had never married James Blood, that because her name was Woodhull, she had simply been his mistress.

Vicky was not the sort of person who lost herself in fantasy. Of course, in a sense, her dream of the Presidency might be called a fantasy, probably the most audacious fantasy a woman could conceive. Still, she had no intention of waiting for some fairy godmother to appear and turn a pumpkin into the White House. Smart enough to realize that she knew nothing about politics, government, or the economy, Vicky began to educate herself.

For the next two years, first in St. Louis, then in Chicago and Pittsburgh, Vicky continued to earn her living by fortune-telling. With her parents and two children to support, she had no other choice. But her evenings were dedicated to the schooling of Victoria Woodhull. In her quest for knowledge, she read the classics, history, philosophy, and economics. Most important, she thought about what she read. She could not swallow whole what others presented as the truth.

Very often, James would suggest problems for her to investigate. Sometimes Vicky would use her psychic powers. Putting herself into a trance, she would come up with proposals for an ideal society, all of which James recorded and saved.

"Working people pay the biggest rents for the worst housing," she once began, pinpointing a problem of slum housing that still exists today. "The first step is to get the workingman out of the city. Small communities of inexpensive cottages could be built in the nearby countryside and cheap trains could carry them back and forth to work each day. With a decent home for his family, a cabbage garden in his backyard, and cheap trains, he could live very well. And I wager he won't want half the beer or whiskey he drinks now."

The subject that preoccupied her, however, was women. "Half of the population do not even possess full rights of citizenship," she declared to James. "There is something terribly wrong with a government that makes women the legal property of their husbands."

He nodded.

Vicky went on. "The whole system needs changing, but men will never make the changes. They have too much to lose."

It was clear to her that the only kind of leader who could begin to make such radical revisions in our political system was a woman. A woman in the White House.

James argued that having a woman ruler did not necessarily mean laws would be changed to benefit women. Reminding Vicky of Queen Victoria, he pointed out that women in England were no better off than women in America.

"Queen Victoria has no sympathy for her own sex," Vicky retorted hotly. "I do. I would encourage American women to disobey the laws until we received justice."

"You are talking treason," James observed.

"No," Vicky corrected. "I'm talking revolution."

And so the nightly sessions went on. In 1868, Vicky and her family were living in Pittsburgh. Late one afternoon, she lounged by the sitting-room fire trying to read the evening paper. Unable to concentrate, she suddenly had an overwhelming feeling that she was not alone. Slowly a figure began to form before her eyes. It was her beautiful young man in the Grecian tunic, the same one who had appeared to her as a child. He began to speak.

"Go to New York City," he said, "to Seventeen Great

Jones Street. There you will find a house ready and waiting for you and yours."

As he spoke, Vicky could see a picture of the house, its outside and then its interior. To the right of the entrance hall was a parlor. A staircase led to the upper floors.

As the vision faded, she could see the young man again. This time she determined not to let him get away.

"Who are you?" she demanded, staring at him with fierce intensity. "All these years, I have never known. Tell me who you are!"

The robed figure reached out and began to write with one finger on a table top. At first Vicky was unable to read the letters. Then the word he had written began to glow. It was a name. DEMOSTHENES.

Two years before, the name Demosthenes would have meant nothing to her. Until she met James, she would not even have known how to pronounce it. Now she recognized it immediately—Demosthenes, the greatest orator of ancient Greece and champion of his country's liberty.

As she struggled to digest what had just happened, the letters on the table quickly faded. Looking up, she realized that Demosthenes was gone.

The next morning she boarded the first train bound for New York City. Number 17 Great Jones Street turned out to be a four-story brownstone in a respectable section of the city. A matronly woman answered her knock.

"Excuse me, ma'am," stammered Vicky, trying to think of an excuse for being there. "Is this house for rent?"

"Why, of course, dear," replied the woman. "We're moving to Buffalo in two weeks. Won't you come in?"

Vicky stepped inside. The hall, the staircase, and the parlor were exactly the same as in her vision. On a table in the parlor, she noticed a book. Stamped in gold on its cover was the title: *The Orations of Demosthenes.* As she later confessed to James, "I was so astonished my blood ran cold!"

4

Queen of Wall Street

Mark Twain called the period following the Civil War America's "Gilded Age." Men like Cornelius Vanderbilt and Andrew Carnegie built incredible fortunes. Railroads crisscrossed the nation. New industries began to mushroom. The industrial revolution, now in full swing, was remaking the country in its own image.

By 1868, New York was one of the liveliest cities in the world. Before the Civil War, Forty-second Street had been a country road. Now the town was booming. Central Park was just beginning to be landscaped. Broadway, the most elegant street, was strung with shops selling jewels, fine imported silks, and the latest bonnets. Along the Bowery, the beer gardens, dance halls, and theaters were crowded with New Yorkers seeking amusement.

Great Jones Street, running between Broadway and the Bowery, was right in the middle of everything. Of course, Vicky thought, the brownstone at Number 17 was hardly the mansion of her prophecy. Nevertheless, it was the most stately house in which she had ever lived. Fortunately, it was large, too, because most of Vicky's family had followed her to New York.

Buck kept pestering her and Tennie to take up fortune-telling quickly before they starved. "Great balls of fire," he would drawl, a familiar glint in his one good eye, "we can make a fortune here. The city is loaded with swells."

But Vicky couldn't concentrate on money. She was too

busy exploring the city. Sometimes she walked around the corner to Lafayette Street where she discovered the fabulous Astor Library. The prophecy had said she would live in a city surrounded by ships. Now, as she strolled along the wharves by the Hudson and East rivers, or peered down into the churning green waters of New York harbor, she felt her destiny close enough to touch.

Bemused, she roamed up one street and down the next. Never had she seen so many churches. It seemed as if each block boasted its own house of worship. On Sunday mornings, it sounded like the whole city was ringing.

At first, Vicky assumed that New York must be a very religious city. Every time she opened a paper, she read about one minister or another. They were the city's celebrities, some of them more famous than stage stars. The best known was Henry Ward Beecher, a stocky man with a mane of gray hair. His emotional sermons could make people laugh or cry. Beecher's pulpit, at Plymouth Church across the river in Brooklyn, was so popular that special ferryboats had to be added on Sundays to accommodate all the worshipers. The boats were known as "Beecher's ferries."

If nearly every block had a church, Vicky soon noticed another common sight. Slowly, she began to doubt the show of godliness and must have murmured angrily to herself, "What hypocrisy!"

For if God were for sale on Sundays, sex was for sale every day of the week. There was nothing secret about the bustling, thriving business of prostitution. The brothels, making themselves as conspicuous as possible, even advertised in the papers.

Strolling on the Bowery, Vicky could also see the street prostitutes, some of them young and well dressed, others aging and desperate. She observed that passersby looked at them with contempt.

One of the preachers' favorite topics for sermons was the evils of prostitution. "Yes," said Vicky to herself, "men sit in church on Sunday and nod their heads in agreement. But who keeps these poor women in business? There would be no prostitution if men did not patronize them."

Then another thought occurred to her. Society insists that women aren't interested in sex. Secretly men take their pleasure with prostitutes; then they turn around and condemn them. Vicky felt no horror at the prostitutes, only waves of pity.

"It's not their fault," she whispered to herself. "Society has doomed them." They were not, after all, so different from other women who offered themselves as sexual objects to lure a man into marriage.

"All of us," fumed Vicky, "are forced to deny we have sexual feelings." Someday, she vowed, people would have to face the truth about women and sex.

Still thinking of the prostitutes, she turned the corner sharply and strode down Great Jones Street.

Buck flew up the front steps at Number 17 and flung himself through the door with such velocity that the parlor windows rattled.

"Vicky!" he bellowed. "Tennie! Everybody!"

At the sound of his shouts, the family began to appear, even fourteen-year-old Byron who squatted in confusion at the top of the staircase.

Beside himself, Buck began to dance madly around the hall, babbling that he had done something extraordinary. Finally he calmed himself sufficiently to make his announcement: he had arranged an appointment for Vicky and Tennie to meet Cornelius Vanderbilt.

The group stared at him in awe, which was precisely the reaction he expected. Nobody needed to ask, "Who is Cornelius Vanderbilt?" He was the richest man in America.

Despite the millions Vanderbilt had made from his vast shipping and railroad empires, he had no use for the things most Americans held dear. He disdained gentlemanly behavior and turned his back on fashionable society. "What do I care about the law?" he had once shouted arrogantly. "Haint I got the power?"

At the age of seventy-six, he did as he liked, which meant playing cards with his cronies and racing his horses at Saratoga. He couldn't stand phonies or people who talked high-falutin. Above all, he hated doctors and ministers. Instead, when his joints began to ache, he consulted a spiritual healer who could relieve his pain by "the laying on of hands." Rather than attend church, he visited a psychic on Staten Island who brought him messages from his dead mother.

These facts about Vanderbilt were common gossip which contributed to his reputation as an eccentric. For Buck, who never stopped scheming to promote his talented daughters, they meant the key to the promised land.

Tennie greeted his announcement with suspicion. Why, she asked, would Commodore Vanderbilt want to meet them?

"Hell, he's a regular fella," roared Buck happily, as if Vanderbilt were already his buddy. "He'll see anybody, so long as they state their business and don't take up too much of his time."

Buck had told Vanderbilt's secretary that one of his daughters could cure any sickness and the other was the best fortune-teller in the world. But Vanderbilt didn't have to take Buck's word. He could see for himself. Buck had also said that his daughters were extremely beautiful.

The next afternoon, Tennie and Vicky carefully dressed in their best outfits. Escorted by a strutting Buck, they walked several blocks northwest to 10 Washington Place, Vanderbilt's red brick house just off Washington Square.

The silver-haired Commodore took a fancy to them immediately, especially to Tennie. "My little sparrow," he was soon calling her affectionately. She, in turn, called him "old boy." With her ivory complexion, cherubic blue eyes and round face wreathed by tawny curls, Tennie looked like an innocent china doll. But, in contrast, she had the kind of personality—irreverent and high-spirited—that her generation found unacceptable in a woman.

Tennie should have been born in the 1920s; she would have made a wonderful "flapper." Bold and impulsive in manner, brash in speech, she generally behaved as she pleased. She acted natural. Other women of her day did not. As a result, Tennie was always shocking people. Vanderbilt happened to be an exception. Probably because the two of them were very much alike, he found her delightful. For Vicky, he felt admiration. While the irrepressible Tennie romped through his mansion, exclaiming over the expensive furnishings, Vicky sat rigid and dignified in a chair. Her quick intelligence, her grave melodic voice, and the delicate beauty of her slender face impressed him greatly. Very often he would ask her for psychic advice on the stock market.

As the visits became more frequent, the friendship between the "old boy" and the two young women grew warmer. Later, people would say that Tennie became his mistress. Probably this was true. In any case, several months after their first meeting, the lonely old man asked twenty-three-year-old Tennie if she would like to become Mrs. Vanderbilt. She refused.

Knowing better than to mention this incredible proposal to her parents, she confided only in her older sister. While Vicky understood the reasons behind Tennie's decision, she nevertheless asked her to consider the offer carefully.

But Tennie had already made up her mind. Not only did she feel that Vanderbilt was too old for her, she also reminded Vicky how much she cherished her freedom.

Neither mentioned the opportunity for financial security Tennie was passing up. It also probably occurred to them that the rejected Commodore might not wish to see them anymore. But the visits went on, and the Commodore continued to reward them generously for their services. In addition to cash, he offered something far better. Suggesting that they use their earnings to buy stock, he began giving them tips on which stocks he thought might do well. When stock prices rose or fell, he advised them on when to sell, when to buy more.

Before long, Vicky and Tennie had a full-time career playing the stock market. Since it was not customary for women to deal directly with brokers, each day James would set off for Wall Street to buy and sell shares for them. Their profits began to accumulate and accumulate.

Life at 17 Great Jones Street began to change dramatically. As the money rolled in, the inhabitants of the house suddenly realized they were wealthy. At least, they certainly acted as though they were. Maids and a cook were hired. A governess was engaged to care for Byron and Zulu Maud. Everyone bought fine new clothes. Roxanna, now a lady of leisure, ordered lace curtains for all the windows and elegant walking suits for herself. Utica filled her wardrobe with low-cut, ruffled gowns in shades of primrose yellow, apple green, and burnt orange. Overnight, Buck transformed himself into a dandy with a clipped beard and expensive leather boots. He began spending most of his time at the racetrack.

Vicky and Tennie seemed to be the only ones who didn't go completely overboard. Vicky's taste had always been conservative; Tennie imitated her. Even though their clothes weren't flashy, they spent a great deal on the finest imported broadcloth, cut and styled into fashionable suits.

Vicky's favorite colors were the purples. The rich shades of plum, violet, lavender, lilac, and mauve accented her pale skin and lustrous blue eyes. She wore no jewelry but would fasten a single white rose on the bodice of her gown or in her hair. Altogether, she cut an impressive figure.

News of the family's sudden affluence soon traveled back to the Midwest. Who should arrive on their doorstep but the two oldest Claflin daughters, Margaret Ann and Polly? Both were divorced, but Polly had remarried. Naturally they brought their entire families with them. The brownstone, which had seemed so spacious a short while ago, now began to shrink. It never occurred to Vicky to send them away. As uneasy as her family made her at times, she always remained loyal.

To support all these relatives in the style to which they were quickly becoming accustomed required a considerable amount of money. But now Vicky and Tennie had it.

Life was not all work. Once a lonely outsider, Vicky began

to make new friends who gave her a sense of belonging. At first, it was James who sought out the city's radicals. When he met interesting people, he'd bring them home. Visionaries, idealists, and reformers soon began to appear at 17 Great Jones Street. The talk was stimulating and lively. Vicky's guests had plenty to say, particularly about politics, government corruption, and the double standard which made one set of rules for women and another for men. Many of the visitors were women—writers, teachers, nurses, lecturers, all of them cultured females.

Vicky's home quickly became a salon, a place where thinking people gathered to discuss the latest ideas and issues. Part of the attraction was the ravishing Vicky herself. Her infectious energy vitalized those who met her. They viewed her as a woman of flaming intelligence, one whose strength of character and personality made her opinions doubly worth hearing. Some people were attracted by her beauty and powers of clairvoyance. Nearly everyone remarked on her musical voice. It sounded like a flute. In everyday conversation, her speech could be fairly ordinary. But when fired to speak on a subject which moved her, her voice seemed to rise from the bottom of her soul.

One evening a new face appeared in her parlor, a tall bearded man named Stephen Pearl Andrews. Vicky worshiped learning, and the sixty-year-old Andrews was the most brilliant person she had ever met. He knew more than James. In fact, the immensity of his knowledge staggered most of his contemporaries.

Andrews spoke thirty languages, including Chinese, and he was trying to develop a universal language which he called "Alwato." An authority on history and government, he had devised a system of world government, a sort of United Nations, which he named the "Pantarchy." A radical committed to social revolution, he believed in socialism, "free love," and feminism. He enjoyed the company of bright women. When his wife, Esther, had studied medicine, Andrews attended classes with her.

It is not surprising that Vicky should have been deeply

impressed by his learning. As for Andrews, he felt an immediate attraction to this woman whose revolutionary ideas paralleled his own. He saw nothing extraordinary about her ambition to be President. Besides, he was shrewd enough to notice that Vicky was rich, very rich. And that she earned the money herself, something few other wealthy women could claim.

If Vicky was smart enough to make a fortune on Wall Street, thought Andrews, she should have no trouble handling the Presidency.

Today, most politicians have their "brain trusts," a small group of valued advisers. In Vicky's day, the idea was not quite so common. Nevertheless, she saw the wisdom in collecting dedicated friends who would work for her cause. James, her first mentor, had been the beginning of her brain trust. Now she added Andrews.

In some ways, Demosthenes had proved correct. In New York City, Vicky became wealthy. Still, much of the prophecy had not happened. She had achieved no fame or even made a start toward her political ambitions. For that matter, outside of her circle of friends, nobody knew she existed. "People won't vote for a nobody," she fretted to herself. Perhaps this feeling that her progress had come to a standstill accounts for what happened next.

One evening, shortly before Christmas, she was entertaining a parlor full of guests. The discussion had turned to women and how they were effectively shut out of the business world. Even two aggressive women like Vicky and Tennie made their financial transactions through James. It had never occurred to them to break tradition by appearing on Wall Street themselves.

"Vicky," somebody called out jokingly, "you and Tennie should start your own brokerage house. Then the men on Wall Street will have to deal with women whether they like it or not."

Another guest took up the theme. "Sure, and they'll have to take off their hats when your carriage drives up!"

Everyone roared with delight at the idea.

Vicky didn't laugh. In fact, the more she thought about it, the more sense it made. Her brain began to click away. She felt positive that the Commodore would help them get started. He was certainly not a feminist, but the idea of backing two women would appeal to his sense of humor.

Of course, the brokerage business was hardly her life's ambition. But it was a beginning. People would notice her. How could they help but take note of the first women brokers in the history of Wall Street?

The next few weeks were busy ones. Vicky and Tennie rented a suite of two rooms on the ground floor of the Hoffman House, a first-class hotel in the Wall Street area. Above all, they wanted to give the impression of being ultra-respectable ladies. This probably accounts for the elaborate way they decorated the suite. There were sofas and easy chairs, oil paintings and sculpture, even a piano.

On the wall, Vicky hung a framed religious motto: Simply to Thy Cross I Cling. Tennie, irreverent as always, decided she'd rather trust in someone she considered more reliable than God. Next to the religious slogan she hung a picture of Commodore Vanderbilt.

Each of them ordered engraved business cards. Vicky's read *Mrs. Victoria C. Woodhull.* Tennie, deciding at the last minute to give herself both a middle initial and a "respectable" married name, called herself *Mrs. Tennie C. Claflin.*

On January 19, 1870, they opened for business. Attention, which Vicky wanted, was immediately forthcoming. Even better, it appeared to be serious, respectful attention. The very next day, a brief article appeared in the New York *Herald:* "The general routine of business in Wall Street was somewhat varied today by the mingling in its scenes of two fashionably dressed ladies as speculators." The item went on to note that nobody seemed to know who the women were or where they had obtained their knowledge of stocks.

Vicky leaped at the opportunity to remedy the situation. She promptly sent off a dignified letter to the *Herald,* coolly implying that their venture was not extraordinary. "We were not a little surprised at seeing our appearance in Wall Street noticed in your columns of yesterday," she wrote. Then, with a superb sense of public relations, she invited the *Herald* to send a reporter around.

As might be expected, the reporter spent most of his column describing the office decor and the sisters' physical appearance. Vicky, he wrote, wore a plain but stylish dress and a rose in her hair. Tennie, who apparently smiled throughout the interview, was pictured as "the photograph of a business woman—keen, shrewd, wholesouled."

No questions were asked about how they had acquired their financial expertise or why they had taken the unprecedented step of opening a brokerage office. If Vicky and Tennie felt excited about attracting the attention of the press, they hid it beautifully. "Cool" was the only word for them.

In the same issue, the *Herald* ran a long editorial titled "Women in Wall Street." It was duly noted that Vicky and Tennie were the first women to invade the all-male sanctuary of the Stock Exchange. Also that their daring action reflected the American woman's growing interest in getting out of the house. After explaining the sociological significance of "the lady brokers," the editorial gallantly concluded by wishing them luck.

In the privacy of their office, Vicky and Tennie could barely contain their rapture. Such enthusiastic words were far more than they had ever hoped for.

As they read the editorial aloud, Vicky stopped at the phrase "lady brokers."

"Do you think that's a way of confessing that male brokers are not always gentlemen?" she giggled.

In every way, their reception was far better than they had anticipated. Tennie went straight out and purchased a scrapbook in which to paste the newspaper clippings. It was to be the first of many clippings and many scrapbooks.

Three weeks later, they moved to more businesslike quarters at 44 Broad Street. This time they launched their new office with a gala opening-day reception. Every newspaper sent reporters. Every brokerage house in the city sent a representative. Businesses in the area closed their doors and hurried over to see what was going on. Even Commodore Vanderbilt put in an appearance.

Before the day was over, four thousand people had thronged through the offices of, as one paper dubbed them, "the Queens of Finance." In fact, the press outdid itself to dream up colorful names—"the Bewitching Brokers," "the She-brokers," "the Female Sovereigns of Wall Street."

There was no doubt that the press adored them. Not only were they a novelty but they also made good copy. Every report commented on the fact that they were very attractive women.

But the papers also were fair enough to describe them as serious businesswomen. Wrote the *Herald*: "Their extraordinary coolness and self-possession, and evident knowledge of the difficult role they have undertaken, is far more remarkable than their personal beauty and graces of manner, and these are considerable."

Initially, the press took them at face value as refined ladies. No reporter asked Vicky, for example, if she was married or where she had been for thirty-two years. Eventually, of course, a few enterprising newspapermen did get around to investigating her background and private life. It is to Vicky's credit that she answered honestly, at least most of the time. The information she did supply had a predictable effect.

Most people were scandalized by her divorce. Her clairvoyance and the tale about Demosthenes brought titters and shakes of the head. Her belief in "free love," only whispered about at this point, also caused offense.

But Vicky paid no attention. She was famous now. Her name—and Tennie's—appeared almost every day in the nation's newspapers. It was all very exciting.

At 44 Broad Street, Vicky looked at her surroundings with deep satisfaction. What a magnificent office, she thought proudly. There were walnut desks covered with green felt and Marvin safes of the highest quality. A sign hung near the front door to discourage the curious who just wanted a peek at the sisters. It read, *All gentlemen will state their business and retire at once.* Outside on the street stood a carriage and driver, always waiting to drive Vicky or Tennie to their appointments.

What a contrast with the life Vicky had led just a year or two ago. Sometimes, sitting at her desk, her thoughts would slip backward—to the darkened parlors where she had told fortunes; to the police pounding on their door with another complaint; to hustling out of Ottawa, Illinois, after Tennie had been indicted for manslaughter when a patient died at Buck's "cancer" clinic. But such grim reminiscing never lasted long. More and more, she banged the lid down hard on her early memories. She preferred to forget. Sometimes, it seemed like those days had never existed.

Vicky enjoyed her work. Although recently James had begun to handle much of the paper work, she sat at her desk in the front office. Brisk and businesslike, she talked to customers, most of them men. Some people on the Street said that she and Tennie were only there for show, that there must be a man behind the scenes doing all the real work. One man tried to give them a forged check, but Vicky immediately spotted the deception and saved the firm a loss of nearly $66,000.

When no customers appeared, Vicky could relax. Lounging behind her desk, she might eat early strawberries and thick fresh cream sent by some friend on the Street. Or she chatted with Buck, who visited nearly every day. Or she cut articles from newspapers and magazines and pasted them into a scrapbook. In those days, a mention in the newspaper supposedly disgraced any woman who wasn't an actress or an agitator. But Vicky loved the press because they were kind to her.

Newspaper articles were a way in which she could measure her success. Seeing her name in print gave her a strange satisfaction. Besides, both she and Tennie enjoyed being interviewed. And the papers loved them because they always had something interesting to say.

One afternoon Vicky told a reporter, "All this talk about women's rights is moonshine!"

He looked surprised. Vicky wasn't finished, though.

"Women have every right," she explained. "All they need to do is exercise them. That's what we're doing. We are doing more for women's rights, by being here on Wall Street, than all the speeches will do in ten years."

If Vicky's statements to the press usually tended to be serious, the reporters knew they could count on Tennie to say something outrageous.

"Miss Tennie," she was asked, "don't you find it embarrassing to work on Wall Street where you are the only woman? People talk about you, you know."

Tennie flung up her arms in disgust. "If I cared about public opinion, I wouldn't leave my house," she retorted defiantly. "The people who gossip about me are powdered dandies and silly crybaby girls. I despise them." Tennie never minced words.

For sentimental reasons, Vicky was attached to the house on Great Jones Street. But with so many freeloading Claflins living there, it had become cramped. Now she could truly afford to live in a mansion and that is precisely what she decided to do. She found an elegant house just off Fifth Avenue in the Murray Hill section of the city. It was even more impressive than Commodore Vanderbilt's house.

She proceeded to decorate her new home in the grandest manner. She bought leaded crystal chandeliers, gothic clocks, carved mahogany tables, gilt chairs, and enormous mirrors which stretched from floor to ceiling. To keep her palace spotless, she hired a battalion of servants. The extravagance worried her, but now she had a home fit for a queen. It might seem a contradiction that Vicky, dedicated to a socialist system that advocated sharing of wealth, would wish to live like a queen. Perhaps this was partly due to the extreme poverty of her early life. Once she was able to afford luxuries, she did not pass them up.

One day, soon after the move to Murray Hill, the maid

announced a visitor. "He won't give his name, ma'am," she reported. "He says he's an old friend of the family's."

From the look of distaste on the maid's face, Vicky knew she was not impressed with the mysterious caller. In fact, she'd left him waiting outside on the doorstep.

Opening the door, Vicky stared in disbelief. There in the chilly February twilight, shivering in a thin suit, stood Canning. She promptly pulled him inside and called a maid to prepare a room. Her former husband looked terribly ill. His face was deathly pale. She discovered that Canning had another problem in addition to alcohol. He had become addicted to a drug, to morphine.

Now forty-six, Canning looked a good twenty years older than his age. After years of abuse, his body had almost burned itself out. Most of the time he played with Byron or wandered around the house in a daze. But he was harmless and bothered nobody. Vicky let him stay.

The return of Canning sparked a fresh wave of gossip. Now people had something far more juicy to whisper about. Mrs. Woodhull, they gasped, was living with both of her husbands!

Vicky may have heard the gossip. Or she may not have. Either way, something far more important was occupying her thoughts. Her "brain trust" had convinced her that the time had come to run for President of the United States.

5

A Different Kind of Woman

On the morning of April 2, 1870, New Yorkers opened
the pages of the *Herald* over their breakfast porridge.
If they got as far as the editorial page, they spotted a letter
to the editor that caused them to shake their heads in
astonishment.

Under the headline *First Pronunciamento* was a historic
bombshell signed by Victoria C. Woodhull. It began, a bit
immodestly, by informing readers that she, Vicky, was "the
most prominent representative of the only unrepresented
class in the Republic."

True, she was one of the most famous women in the land.
But her statement would do little to endear her to Susan
B. Anthony and others who had been fighting for women's
rights when Vicky was reading fortunes in the Middle West.
Vicky didn't mean to insult the feminist leaders. She simply
felt their route to equality was not very effective. Action, not
talk, was her solution.

She went on to say, "While others argued the equality
of women with men, I proved it by successfully engaging in
business." Here again was her contention that women have
the same rights as men; they just don't use them.

Then she got to the point: "I now announce myself
candidate for the Presidency."

Aware of the stir her letter would create, she hastened to
assure the public that she was not a crackpot.

"I anticipate criticism," she wrote, "but however

unfavorable the comment this letter may evoke, I trust that my sincerity will not be called into question.

"I have deliberately and of my own accord placed myself before the people as a candidate for the Presidency of the United States, and having the means, courage, energy and strength necessary for the race, intend to contest it to the close."

Money, courage, strength—these she possessed. But there was one essential for election that she did not mention because she did not have it—manhood.

The next national election would not be held until 1872. Nevertheless, James and Stephen advised that she would need two years to establish herself in the minds of the voters. One of the chief subjects discussed by her "brain trust" did not concern politics at all. It had to do with reeducating the men of this country, the ones who cast the ballots. Very, very few men approved of women in public life. They believed women belonged in the home, preferably in the kitchen. Most women agreed.

The great political parties did not take women seriously. After all, a woman couldn't even vote. A woman on the ticket would be more than a liability. It would be a joke.

In 1870 Ulysses S. Grant, a Republican and a Civil War hero, occupied the White House. Nobody doubted that the popular general would run for a second term in the 1872 election. The Democrats had no idea whom they would nominate, but it certainly wouldn't be a female. There were other, smaller parties, too. But they weren't crazy about women candidates either.

The only way a woman could hope to compete was to nominate herself. With luck, she might marshal enough public support to get her name on the ballot.

Did Victoria Woodhull really believe that she had a chance to win? The answer is yes.

One reason she felt her cause far from hopeless was the prophecy. Hadn't Demosthenes insisted that she would lead her people? This powerful belief in her destiny gave her faith and a sense of self-confidence which proved contagious.

James and Stephen believed in her because she believed so strongly in herself. In those days, some unlikely people had managed to become President. Where had Abraham Lincoln been before his nomination? Practicing law in an obscure Illinois town. Certainly the notion of a woman President sounded strange. But no woman had ever tried before. Just possibly she might succeed.

Looking back, Vicky's campaign must be rated as one of the most carefully thought-out in American political history. She did everything right, up to a point that is. Announcing her candidacy was only the first step. She had no intention of stopping there. People already knew that she was a wealthy, self-made woman; now she had to make the entire country aware of the socialistic principles for which she stood.

She began to write a series of essays about politics and government which later would be published as a book, *The Principles of Government*. The essays, appearing first in the New York *Herald*, were much too scholarly for the average reader. But they succeeded in giving Vicky a new image. People couldn't help but conclude that Mrs. Woodhull was a learned woman, a person who had the intelligence and qualifications to be President. In that way, the essays served a useful purpose.

The dream in sight at last, Vicky felt a sense of jubilation. Still, she knew that hardly anybody cheered the announcement of her candidacy. Oh, her friends had hurried over to the brokerage office to offer congratulations. And a few newspapers took her seriously. One editorial remarked that her candidacy was notable for its novelty and courage. "Now for Victory for Victoria in 1872!" it said.

Another paper pointed out that she was a smart and handsome woman. Therefore, "she is the proper person to stand forth against the field as the woman's rights candidate for the White House."

But other papers sneered. The "weaker sex," they said, already have plenty of privileges. Women should be happy with what they have. The obvious was mentioned—that men would never accept a woman President.

Finally, the press got around to saying what really bothered them. The men who wrote newspaper editorials were pretty much like most people in the country, and most people believed it was unnatural for a woman to govern.

As news of Vicky's candidacy traveled across the country, people began to talk about her. Over steins of ale in the taverns, men asked what the world was coming to. Some felt sure that she must be a homely, man-eating spinster with a cat. Only that type of woman would make a public spectacle of herself. Other men said she must be a beautiful courtesan. Only that type of woman would call attention to herself.

Over their teacups, the women also gossiped about her. Vicky intrigued them. They wanted to know all about her, but what they learned made them uneasy. She might be rich and beautiful, but she also sounded unfeminine. No true woman would demean herself by running for political office. This woman, so different from themselves, troubled them.

Those who had the most trouble with Vicky's new prominence were the Claflins. Tennie, as usual, thought anything her sister did must be wonderful. She was busy clipping newspapers. But the rest of the family scoffed and sulked. The one who felt most put out was Roxanna.

"Where do you get these fancy ideas?" she would screech at Vicky. She placed the blame on her son-in-law.

"It's that hellhound Blood who put you up to it," Roxanna squawked. "Blood and Andrews and that passel of free lovers hangin' around here. I reckon they bewitched you!"

At first, Roxanna had liked money and new clothes. But after a while she began to loathe living in New York. She felt lost. Nor did she like Vicky's friends. Her ambition for her daughters was for them to catch rich husbands and drive around in their own carriages. She ignored the fact that Vicky could afford her own carriage.

Vicky no longer listened to her mother's advice. Neither did Tennie, who now went along with everything Vicky did. Roxanna thought longingly of the wagon trips zigzagging through the Midwest, telling fortunes and selling "Miss

Tennessee's Magnetic Elixir." To her mind, those were the happy days.

When Vicky asked Polly and her family to leave so that Stephen Pearl Andrews could move in, there were more scenes. Roxanna stormed and carried on. Finally, with much bitterness, Polly departed.

The feminists should have been happy about Vicky's announcement. But they ignored her. She was not one of them. All they knew about her was what they read in the papers, and, frankly, they were not impressed. In truth, they felt resentful. A woman running for President? None of them had dared to dream on so grand a scale. Their most radical demand was the right to vote. The feminists had never actually thought about women running for political office.

As Vicky went to work altering the thinking of America, her biggest obstacle turned out to be another woman named Victoria. At that time, Queen Victoria was the most powerful monarch on earth. Her reign, which lasted sixty-four years from 1837 to 1901, was called the Victorian Age. People who lived then, both in England and in America, were called Victorians. That period of history is known for being stuffy, dull, and narrow-minded.

In a way, Queen Victoria regarded herself as a freak of nature. Although she did a man's job, she had a good excuse —she had inherited the throne. In all other cases, she did not approve of women working outside the home. In her daily life, she carried out the duties of queen as well as those of wife and mother.

Not surprisingly, she hated the whole idea of women's rights. The notion of women doctors especially shocked her. "The idea of allowing young girls and young men to enter the dissecting room together," she wrote to her prime minister, "is awful." She underlined "awful."

But the queen didn't dislike women. In one area she sympathized greatly with her own sex. When she thought of "us poor women" being exploited by sex-mad husbands, she simply fumed. Sex was a part of life the queen gladly would have done without.

People in those days had a special way of looking at women. The Victorian woman was not supposed to be a mere human being. She was better—she was an angel. Even women thought so.

A popular novel, written by a woman, had this to say: "God, the Maker, tenderly anchored womanhood in the peaceful, blessed haven of home; and if man is ever insane enough to mar the divine economy, by setting women afloat on the turbulent, roaring sea of politics, they will speedily become pitiable wrecks." Flowery, but that's how women saw themselves. They expected men to treat them reverently.

Since women were supposed to be delicate creatures, they often had fainting spells, sick headaches, and a host of nervous disorders. Blushing was fashionable. Sex was never discussed, and if a woman enjoyed it, she didn't say so. Modesty became a cult. When women went to doctors, they often were too shy to say what part of their bodies hurt. For the sake of fashion, they wore corsets so tightly laced they could barely breathe and layers of skirts and petticoats weighing up to twelve pounds.

A refined girl had only one purpose in life—to find a husband. She was educated and trained for the marriage market. Once she had achieved her goal, she spent the rest of her life in the home, raising her children and obeying her husband. The vast majority of marriages were minor disasters, but few women rebelled. In 1867 there were only 9937 divorces in the whole country.

The Victorian woman understood the rules, and she played by them.

Then there was Victoria Woodhull, the "new woman." Her most redeeming feature, in the opinion of her contemporaries, was her beauty. She had a classic aquiline profile on the left side of her face—her right profile was a bit irregular—and a lithe, graceful body. Her hair, once long, was now cropped short like a boy's, a fashion considered daring and extreme.

Unlike most women in the nineteenth century, Vicky was athletic and enjoyed sports. She knew how to ride a horse, row a boat, swim, dance, and play billiards. She could walk all day and never had been known to faint or blush.

The last place Vicky wanted to spend her time was at home. The Victorian world, however, was not geared for dealing with a woman who appeared in public, at least not without a male at her side for protection. One evening shortly before seven p.m., Vicky and Tennie left the brokerage office and decided to eat dinner at a restaurant. They chose Delmonico's, New York's most popular French restaurant. No strangers to the place, they had lavishly entertained customers there on many occasions.

Settling at a table, Vicky ordered their first course. "Tomato soup for two, please," she said.

The waiter coughed nervously but didn't move.

"Why don't you get the soup?" she asked.

Looking uncomfortable, the waiter shuffled his feet. "Beg pardon, madam, but it's after six and there is no gentleman with you."

Tennie was getting hungry and angry. "You go and send Charlie Delmonico to us," she instructed the waiter.

A few moments later, the apologetic owner appeared at their table. Charles Delmonico admired the sisters. He also valued their patronage. But rules were rules. And custom was custom.

"I can't let you eat here without a man," he said lamely.

Vicky surveyed him coolly. "Why not?" She knew perfectly well that women couldn't be served after six without an escort.

"It would start an awful precedent," said Delmonico. "All kinds of women would come in here alone. It would cause all sorts of embarrassment."

"We certainly don't want to embarrass you," said Tennie, barely keeping the sarcasm from her voice.

Giving Vicky a mischievous wink, she rose and marched to the door. Outside she waved to the driver who was waiting for them atop their carriage.

"Get down off your box and come in here," she yelled.

By this time, everyone in the restaurant was standing up, watching.

Tennie paraded the red-faced man down the aisle and pulled out a chair. After he had been seated, Vicky again summoned the waiter.

"Tomato soup for three," she said.

This incident, and others, added to her legend. Tales about her circulated all over the country. No matter how bizarre the stories, people believed them.

Shortly after the opening of her brokerage house, she had asked a newspaper reporter not to flatter her. "I am a businesswoman," she had declared heatedly. "Treat me as fairly as you do men. That is all I ask." She didn't want favors because of her sex.

Now she demanded no special treatment as a candidate. As she knew quite well, every politician was open to criticism, sometimes nasty criticism. She would just have to live with it.

Sometimes Vicky was asked why she wanted to be President. That question utterly mystified Victorians, who believed all women were content at home. They couldn't understand why a woman should want to subject herself to the spittoons and cigar smoke of all-male politics. In this instance, Vicky did not answer with her customary honesty.

"I want to draw the public's attention to women's claims that we are the political equals of men," she usually said. This sounded good, and it even may have been partly true. She did believe that women should participate in the serious affairs of the nation. But there was another reason that made her run: she wanted to be President.

These days, Vicky was feeling elated. She found herself humming, something she rarely did. Somehow she knew that Demosthenes could not be wrong. One afternoon a reporter from the New York *Sun* came to interview her at home. Sitting decorously in the drawing room, she answered questions with her usual seriousness. The reporter, however, seemed to be more interested in her wardrobe than in her political views.

Suddenly Vicky jumped up. "Let me show you a dress I intend to wear someday," she said.

Ten minutes later, she reappeared.

The reporter blinked. Vicky was wearing navy knee-length pants, buckled at the knees. Under them she had powder-blue stockings which revealed her shapely legs. On top, she wore a dark-blue blousy tunic which ended above the knees and a white shirt with a tie.

For a moment, there was silence from the embarrassed newspaperman.

"Mrs. Woodhull," he finally blurted out, "if you appear on the street in that dress, the police will arrest you."

Vicky drew herself up angrily. "No, they won't," she declared. "When I'm ready to make my appearance in this dress, no policeman will touch me."

She had chosen it for her inauguration. She knew that the President of the United States is not likely to be arrested.

"It must be a newspaper for intelligent women," Vicky insisted in as firm a voice as she could muster. She and Tennie were seated around a large table in the library with James, Stephen and a newly added adviser, Dr. Joseph Treat. The room reeked of cigar smoke.

"Are you forgetting that women can't vote?" James replied in a teasing tone.

For weeks, the group had been meeting to discuss strategies by which Vicky might promote her campaign. By now it was clear that she was not getting sufficient coverage in the daily newspapers. Her essays on politics and finance had been admirably conceived but, unfortunately, few people read them. Besides they told little about Vicky as a person. What she needed was a forum in which to express her ideas.

The one suggestion everybody liked was to publish a weekly newspaper. But what kind of newspaper? James and Stephen favored a liberal journal that would appeal to any modern-thinking person, regardless of sex. Their basic purpose, after all, was to get male votes. The paper must interest men, and it certainly couldn't afford to offend them. Vicky disagreed.

"Of course the purpose of a newspaper would be to support me for the Presidency," she admitted. "But I've seen the campaign sheets put out by other candidates. They're cheap rags, used the next day for kindling fires."

Rising from her chair, she walked over to the window and stared out at the gas lamps on Thirty-eighth Street. Besides, the usual campaign sheets were dreadfully boring. Who wanted to read page after page of laudatory comments about the candidate? Her paper would be a first-class journal, with lively articles directed toward women.

Turning back to the table, she said decisively, "Reform, radicalism, and feminism. Those are the basic themes."

"What! No revolution?" Tennie said with a short laugh.

Everyone at the table had read the feminist newspaper published by Susan Anthony and Elizabeth Cady Stanton. It was called *The Revolution*. Vicky had run a few ads for the brokerage firm in *The Revolution*, but she did not intend to use it as her model. In her opinion, the contents appeared far from revolutionary. They were dull and badly written.

"Excuse me, has anyone seen *The Woman's Journal?*" Dr. Treat asked.

Vicky grimaced. This was another feminist paper published by Lucy Stone and other conservatives in the women's movement. Its contents were so mild and timid that Vicky regarded the paper as ineffectual.

She seated herself at the table again. "If we are to publish a paper," she said with quiet authority, "it must reflect my views and my concerns. I am a woman; most of my concerns involve my own sex. It will be a woman's paper, but if the articles are stimulating and timely, they should appeal to men as well."

So the decision for a woman's paper was made. The discussion moved to what kind of articles they would print. Tennie seemed to have more ideas than anyone.

In fact, she offered to write a series of articles about prostitution. There was a dead silence while the men stared at her. They had not been aware that Tennie wanted to be part of the paper. Nor did they believe that she had any writing ability.

"Since when have you become a writer?" Stephen asked bluntly.

Tennie looked at him sharply. "Since when does a person need a lot of fancy degrees to write a clear English sentence?" she demanded.

Dr. Treat felt there was no reason to antagonize readers with such a sensational topic.

Vicky glanced at him with contempt, declaring that prostitution was a feminist subject and one they should certainly cover. Perhaps it was not a suitable topic for their first issue but, later on, yes.

As the meeting was about to adjourn, James suddenly realized that they had forgotten something important—what to call the journal.

Vicky smiled at her sister. "Since Tennie is going to be at my side once more, I say we should call it *Woodhull and Claflin's Weekly*."

6

Crusading Publisher

Spring arrived in New York. With it came *Woodhull and Claflin's Weekly* and a new phase of Vicky's life. She was now a publisher, not the first or only woman to own her own newspaper but certainly one of the few.

On May 14, 1870, Volume One, Number One, appeared on the city's newsstands. Above the masthead was emblazoned the paper's motto, Upward and Onward. The first issue of sixteen pages looked impressive. Printed on the finest-quality paper, it had the look of a classy journal, not a fly-by-night campaign sheet.

Inside could be found a variety of lively articles. There was the first installment of a new novel by the controversial French writer who called herself "George Sand," chatty theater and book reviews, sports scores, a financial column, and a fashion section. An entire page was devoted to poetry. For example:

> Are Statesmen vain enough to think
> That they would have been free
> If woman had not lent her hand
> And fought for liberty?

One poem instructed women in the meaning of the latest slang, a subject ordinarily off-limits to "ladies."

Much of the contents was devoted to news about women: a profile of Elizabeth Cady Stanton, fiftieth-birthday greetings to Susan B. Anthony, and several articles about the political rights women did not yet have. The tone of the entire newspaper was strongly pro-woman. Even by today's standards, it would be called a radical feminist paper. One might expect that such a paper would not be warmly greeted in that conservative period. However, response turned out to be favorable, probably because the *Weekly* was so well written and professionally produced.

Vicky printed 50,000 copies of the first issue and made sure that newspapers throughout the country received complimentary copies. "A handsome and readable paper," commented the New York *Standard*. "Undoubtedly the ablest journal of its class and can hardly fail of success," said the Philadelphia *Day*.

From the beginning, Vicky had realized that publishing would be an expensive venture. Printing and distribution costs ran high, and the same was true for the spacious office she had leased at 21 Park Row. But she had her own personal money to spend plus the profits from the brokerage firm which was doing well. Still, she tried to make the *Weekly* self-supporting. She solicited subscriptions at $3 a year until, eventually, the *Weekly* had 20,000 subscribers all over the country. The front page carried paid announcements for New York's most reputable bankers and brokers. Advertisements for wine and liquor dealers and billiard parlors were run on the inside pages. Vicky refused to accept advertising from abortionists and brothels.

She had no expense for writers. Many of the articles she wrote herself; but she could also count on James, Stephen, and her intellectual friends, who were eager to contribute.

Some of the finest essays were produced by Tennie, who was turning into an amazingly clear feminist thinker and writer. In one article, for instance, she urged women to gain their sexual freedom by defying oppressive social customs. Attacking the double standard, she wrote, "A free man is a noble being; a free woman is a contemptible being." Not until women are unafraid of being called nasty names by men will there be true liberation, she concluded.

Over the months, the *Weekly* gradually became more radical. Women could still read about a female contractor in New Hampshire or a postmistress at West Point, but the paper also began to expose insurance frauds and bond swindles. It analyzed strikes by the coal workers and advocated labor unions for workers. Later, it would be the first newspaper in the United States to print the Communist Manifesto.

The area in which it pioneered, however, was sexuality. If anything infuriated Vicky, it was hypocrisy. The Victorian era happened to be an extremely hypocritical period of history, and nowhere was there more deception than in matters of sex.

On the surface, Victorians appeared to be genteel, mannerly, and proper. Underneath, behavior was often strikingly different. Men insisted that women remain pure and virginal. At the same time, it was common to have a mistress or patronize a prostitute.

In public, prostitution was attacked as a great evil. This was a favorite theme for the Reverend Henry Ward Beecher. One of his most popular sermons, "The Strange Woman," described venereal disease in lurid detail. "Every year, in every town," intoned Beecher from his pulpit at Plymouth Church, "die wretches scalded and scorched with agony."

In private, prostitution was tolerated. Indeed, it was a big business. There were over twenty thousand prostitutes in New York City alone.

Bishop Simpson of the Methodist Episcopal Church claimed that there were as many prostitutes in New York as there were Methodists. The superintendent of police called this an exaggeration, but he did admit that the city had 621 houses of prostitution, 96 houses of assignation where a man and woman could meet to rent a room, and 75 dance halls where "women of ill repute" hung out. In addition, there was no way of counting the women who roamed the streets.

What everybody knew, but nobody admitted, was that a man with money could find a woman at any time of day or night. Vicky ran articles exposing this situation when no other publication dared to mention it. She published the names of those who owned houses of prostitution, and these included respectable citizens and even churches. She described the conditions under which prostitutes had to work and how little of their earnings they kept. Payoffs to the police were noted as well.

Vicky believed that prostitutes were victims. Since prostitution could probably not be eliminated, she wanted it to be legalized. Most of the evils would be lessened, she thought, if brothels were licensed by the police and inspected regularly by doctors.

The *Weekly* discussed other unmentionable topics: birth control, abortion, venereal disease, and female sexual response. In an age when many women were so modest that they would not permit a doctor to examine them, the *Weekly* blasted such prudery and advised women to learn about their bodies.

On top of all this, Vicky openly avowed her belief in sexual freedom for women and crusaded for a single, not double, standard of morality for both women and men. The public lumped together her writings about sex into one category: "free love." Eventually she would have a reputation for being a notorious "free lover." "Respectable" citizens thought she was horrible.

Vicky was not the first woman to speak of female sexuality. Before her had been the English feminist Mary Wollstonecraft, who lived with two men without being married. In the late 1700s, she had argued that when a woman and man no longer feel strong physical attraction for each other, their relationship should end. After Vicky would come the birth-control pioneer, Margaret Sanger. Both these women fared better with the public than Vicky, who had the misfortune to live in a prudish age.

In her time, Vicky was the only feminist to see the connection between feminism and sexual freedom. Others, like Elizabeth Cady Stanton, believed women should have the same privileges as men, but their private lives were models of Victorian respectability.

* * *

It was now the summer of 1870. Although only June, the scorched city already baked under a heat wave. Vicky began arriving at the *Weekly* office earlier so that she could work in the morning coolness. At her desk, she dipped her pen into the inkwell; but the fresh, white sheet of paper before her remained empty. Her eyes kept moving to a letter she had received a few days ago. It demanded a reply, but Vicky could think of none.

"Dear Mrs. Woodhull," the brief note read. "Will you ask Demosthenes if there is any new argument not yet made on the 14th and 15th Amendments that he will bring out through some of us at the coming convention?" And it was signed Elizabeth Cady Stanton.

Although the *Weekly* had been on the stands for nearly six weeks, this was the first personal word she had received from anyone in the women's movement. Vicky felt a bit hurt when they had completely ignored the new paper. But Mrs. Stanton sounded like a kind, friendly woman.

After the Civil War, the slaves had received their freedom. The Fourteenth and Fifteenth Amendments to the Constitution had granted black males the right to vote. For the past several years, the feminists had focused nearly all their attention on these two amendments. Could they be interpreted to include females? Would it be necessary to add another amendment to the Constitution to ensure women the ballot? The feminists were still laboring to find the right answer. At their annual convention coming up in January, they planned to devote almost the entire agenda to this question.

Reading the note again, Vicky suddenly wondered if Mrs. Stanton could be mocking her. Why should Demosthenes give new ideas to Mrs. Stanton and her friends? They pretended she didn't exist. Full of bitterness for a moment, Vicky said to herself, "If Demosthenes helps anyone, it will be me."

That steaming evening, she climbed to the roof of her Murray Hill mansion. Almost nightly she came up here to escape the noisy Claflin brood, to meditate, pray, and think in peace. Above her head the velvet sky was dotted with stars. She looked down on the quiet blackness below and saw the branches of trees shining by the gleam of the street lamps.

Slowly Vicky could feel herself relaxing. Since that morning she had read over the amendments so often that she knew them by heart.

"All persons born or naturalized in the United States . . . are citizens of the United States. . . . No State shall make or enforce any law which shall abridge the privileges or immunities of citizens of the United States. . . . The right of citizens of the United States to vote shall not be denied or bridged . . . on account of race, color, or previous condition of servitude."

"All persons, all persons, . . ." she repeated to herself hypnotically. Perhaps the answer might be hidden in those two words. Suddenly a thought flashed into her mind. The amendments clearly stated that all persons were citizens, and all citizens had the right to vote. Were not women "persons"? The male legislators who had drafted the amendments were not thinking of women when they wrote those sentences. Probably they did not regard women as persons.

"But, of course, we are," Vicky thought excitedly. "Our right to vote may not be spelled out but surely it is implied."

Was an implication good enough? She was unsure. Lying on her back, staring up at the Big Dipper, she decided to say nothing to others for the moment. The matter deserved more thought.

Vicky did not forget her definition of "persons" in the Fourteenth and Fifteenth Amendments. The idea continued to simmer at the back of her mind.

One night in September, she gave a lavish party. That night the mansion, brilliantly lit, looked like a fairyland. Reflected in the parquet floors was the gleam of wax candles in their cut-glass chandeliers. Her guests danced the Virginia reel and the Spanish fandango. Later, there would be refreshments—ice cream and cakes and beautiful glace fruits.

Someone took her arm. "Vicky, I would like to present a friend, the Honorable Benjamin Butler." Extending her hand in welcome, Vicky bowed graciously.

Mr. Butler was so short that she had to bend down to converse with him. She thought she had never met anyone quite so ugly. He was stout, bald, and his spindly legs made him look like a dwarf.

She fought back a smile. This quaint little man had been an important general during the Civil War; indeed, in the South, he still had a reputation for being cruel and bloodthirsty. Once, when some southern women refused to greet him by turning their backs on him, he had joked, "They know which end of them looks best." His lack of gallantry earned him the nickname "Beast Butler."

A lawyer by profession, Butler was now a member of Congress. He also sat on the powerful House Judiciary Committee, the congressional committee that ruled on all petitions requesting a change in the nation's laws.

Vicky immediately drew Congressman Butler to one side. While carefully outlining her thoughts on the Fourteenth and Fifteenth Amendments, she discovered several encouraging facts about her guest. He sympathized with the feminist cause. He believed her interpretation of the amendments was valid. What's more, he seemed eager to help her.

This eagerness to help was not unusual in Vicky's relationships with men. It did not always endear her to women. In fact, Susan Anthony once remarked that she didn't trust Victoria Woodhull because she surrounded herself with men. "She is wholly owned and dominated by men-spirits," Susan said. Nobody "owned and dominated" Vicky; but in some respects, it was a fair comment. Vicky's beauty and intelligence—a kind of magnetism she had—drew men to her. They fell all over themselves to be of service. Rarely did she refuse.

Butler now busily described the steps Vicky might take. He suggested that she draft a special petition called a Memorial. Any person or group believing a law was unjust could present their grievances to Congress in this manner.

If the nation's legislators thought the Memorial had merit, eventually the unjust law would be changed.

Once Vicky had written down her legal arguments, Butler added, she should send them to the House Judiciary Committee where he would see that they got prompt and serious attention.

Privately, Butler doubted that his colleagues on the Committee would approve Vicky's radical interpretation. Most of them tended to be stuffy and conservative. But Butler believed it worth a try. Perhaps if the congressmen met the dashing Vicky, they would be more favorably impressed by her theories.

"My dear, I have an idea," he declared enthusiastically, thinking aloud as he spoke. "Sometimes, on rare occasions, a petitioner is invited to personally address Congress on the subject of his Memorial. I might be able to arrange for you to appear."

As Vicky listened to Congressman Butler, she could hardly believe her good fortune. Here was a man who had just walked into her drawing room, unannounced, and handed her the key to the Congress. Was there no end to her luck?

"Mr. Butler, I would be so grateful," she exclaimed.

"Well, my dear, I cannot promise you," he warned. "After all, a woman has never addressed Congress before. We might run into a slight problem there. But I assure you that I will do my best."

Later, after her guests had departed, Vicky climbed to the roof. It was a clear, chilly night, the sky so full of stars she couldn't begin to count them. She wanted to reach up on tiptoe and grasp a whole handful—Orion and Polaris and still higher, the Pleiades.

Arching her neck upward, she began to smile. Recently she had read a statement saying that participation in politics would excite women to the point of insanity. What nonsense! Did Catherine II of Russia go mad? Did Anne of Austria? Speaking for herself, Vicky had never felt saner. Never had she held her future so firmly in her own two hands.

At the same time, though, she felt vaguely disturbed.

She was sadly aware that her relations with her family had grown thin and strained. Much of the romance she had once known with James had turned stale. They were still friends, comrades, and business partners. But rarely lovers, even though she loved him more deeply than any other man she had ever known.

More and more these days, she found herself turning to nine-year-old Zulu Maud. She felt strangely comforted by her daughter's presence. The girl had grown into a quiet child, solemn and patient beyond her years, who was always offering to do small chores for her mother. Vicky wished she could spend more time with Zulu Maud because it was clear the lonely child did not really enjoy her boisterous Claflin relatives.

Byron had been lost to her for many years. Rarely did he acknowledge her presence. Instead, he preferred the company of his father. The sixteen-year-old boy's body had almost matured into manhood, bur his mind dwelt in other spheres. Canning was also lost in a hazy world of alcohol and drugs. Father and son clung to each other.

Over the months, Roxanna had worked herself into such a sulk that sometimes Vicky wished she could ship her back to the Midwest. Instead of directing her bad temper at Vicky, though, she took out her frustrations on James. Provoking needless arguments over nothing, she began to needle James about earning his living from Vicky and Tennie. Roxanna conveniently overlooked the fact that, between the brokerage firm and the newspaper, James often put in a twelve-hour workday.

When quarrels broke out in the household, as they did frequently, all of Vicky's sisters except Tennie sided with Roxanna. Although Vicky supported them, as well as their children, they bore her no gratitude or affection. For many years, she had tried to win their love. Now she realized it was impossible. Jealous and sullen, they could never accept her success or prominence.

Vicky spent many long hours writing and rewriting her Memorial for Congress. Consulting a stack of law books, she struggled to present her arguments as convincingly as possible. When she had finished in November, she decided to send up a trial balloon to test public reaction. Running a short article in the *Weekly* under the attention-getting headline *Startling Annunciation*, she briefly summarized her theory that the Fourteenth and Fifteenth Amendments gave women the right to vote. Then she sat back to wait.

To her dismay, she received almost no response. One newspaper sarcastically dismissed her idea as foolishness.

In a sense, Vicky's article was a belated reply to Mrs. Stanton's letter of the previous summer. Surely, she thought, Mrs. Stanton would contact her again. But Vicky had no word from Mrs. Stanton or from any of the feminists. Did they, too, consider her silly?

Finally, it was Tennie who reported the gossip going around feminist circles. "They say it was Butler's idea! Guess they don't think you're smart enough."

Quivering, Vicky managed a tense smile.

"They reject my argument because they don't like me," she replied. "What fools and hypocrites they are. All their talk of sisterhood! They only want to be sisters with respectable ladies like themselves."

At that time, nearly all the feminists were middle-class, educated women. Their rebellion against the low status of women was mainly intellectual. They were fortunate enough to lead comfortable lives. None had suffered from poverty or physical drudgery. None was divorced. None had worked to support her children.

Vicky had a real knowledge of woman's oppression because she had lived it. Unlike the feminist leaders, she had never been sheltered from the harsh realities of life. Unquestionably, this accounts for much of her radical approach to feminism.

Now, her feelings battered, she began to hate the women's movement. "They talk about women's rights but when a woman uses her rights, they spit on her," she fumed. "They think they're too good to associate with me." For a moment, she felt very small and insignificant.

In December, Vicky boarded a train for Washington to deliver her Memorial to Congress. Waiting at the station with good news was Congressman Butler. On January 11, she would be addressing the House Judiciary Committee. The "Queen of Prostitutes," as some newspapers were now calling her, would be the first woman to receive this honor.

7
Victoria and the Feminists

Isabella Beecher Hooker was suspicious and very, very upset. Earlier in the day, several hundred feminists had begun arriving in Washington for the annual January convention of the National Woman's Suffrage Association. Isabella, the organizer of the convention, already had had enough trouble trying to arrange for speakers. She had failed so miserably that Susan Anthony returned early from a lecture tour to straighten out the mess.

Now this, she thought, as she stared at the newspaper on her lap. There, in black and white, was a report that Victoria Woodhull would address the House Judiciary Committee tomorrow morning, January 11, 1871. Her appearance was set for ten a.m., exactly the same time as the opening of the convention. Although this was entirely a coincidence, Isabella suspected that Vicky had arranged it deliberately.

Meeting later at teatime with Susan, Pauline Davis, and other feminists, Isabella could not contain her anger. Nor could the others, who seemed to forget all about the convention. They could talk of nothing but Mrs. Woodhull.

Not surprisingly, they remembered the gossip they'd heard about Vicky: she was divorced; she lived with both her husbands; she entertained radicals and "free lovers"; she held orgies.

One woman brought up the unconventional Tennie and her relationship with Commodore Vanderbilt.

"She's a bold one," said Isabella. "They say she smokes cigars."

What disturbed them most was Vicky's coup. None of the feminists had been invited to address Congress. How had an immoral woman like Victoria Woodhull managed to achieve this great honor? Their cries of outrage mounted to a crescendo.

Finally Susan Anthony made a suggestion. "Why don't we attend the committee hearing tomorrow and find out what she has to say?"

"Certainly not," retorted Isabella obstinately. "I would never associate with that woman nor will I contaminate myself by listening to her speak." The others fluttered in agreement.

The group was meeting at the home of Senator Samuel Pomeroy where Isabella was a house guest. Susan suggested that they ask the senator from Kansas for his opinion.

As it happened, Senator Pomeroy had no sympathy with their agitation.

"This is not the way politics works," he told them bluntly. "Men could never work in a political party if they stopped to investigate each member's background. If you are going into a fight, you must accept all the help you can get."

Swallowing their pride, the feminists decided to postpone their convention until the next afternoon.

January 11 was a typical Washington winter day, sunny and fairly mild. Arriving early at the Capitol with Tennie and James, Vicky nervously clutched a copy of her speech— "Further Arguments in Support of Victoria Woodhull's Memorial." Soon the marble corridor outside the hearing room began to fill up. Clerks hurried through the crowd carrying sheafs of papers and documents. Congressmen assembled in small groups, peeping at Vicky out of the corners of their eyes. Also waiting in the corridor were three stern-looking women—Susan Anthony, Isabella Beecher Hooker, and Pauline Davis.

Vicky recognized Susan immediately, but the other faces were not familiar. Fearful of meeting their eyes, she continued talking to Tennie. It would be impossible for her to speak to them. From the frosty expressions on their faces, she could read their feelings about her.

Actually, the women were gaping at Vicky more in disbelief than in disapproval. Until this morning, they had never seen her in person, and they had difficulty believing their eyes.

"Why, she looks like a lady!" declared Isabella in a shocked whisper.

Vicky wore a tasteful plum-colored gown with a white rose at her throat. Her face, framed by short curly hair, looked sad. In truth, she was scared to death.

James had been quietly circulating through the crowd to hear what people were saying about Vicky. Now he returned to her side.

"One of those women over yonder must be the Reverend Beecher's sister," he reported. "I overheard her say that she had no intention of speaking to you. Then a gentleman told her that a Beecher should be the last person to criticize you because—are you listening?—because her brother preaches to at least twenty of his mistresses every Sunday. What do you think that means?"

"Oh, James," Vicky answered sharply. "How should I know?"

All she could think of was her coming ordeal. Simply being there made her feel awestruck. Suddenly her childhood inferiority swept over her again. She was a nobody. Her family were trash. Respectable folks looked down on her.

The doors to the committee room stood open now, and people began filing in. As she looked around, Vicky thought, "None of these people likes me or wishes me well, except Mr. Butler." Her impulse was to turn and walk out.

It was time for the hearing to begin. Vicky heard herself being introduced. As she rose to her feet, she felt her hands grow moist with perspiration. This was the first public speech she had ever made, and as she opened her mouth, the words came out in a whisper. Someone asked her to repeat because she couldn't be heard.

Quietly she began to read her speech, outlining her legal arguments to prove that the Constitution already gave women the right to vote. Gradually her voice grew stronger and more dramatic. But by bit, her nervousness fled; the words began to tumble out. Her cheeks grew flushed and her eyes sparkled.

"Women, white and black, belong to races, although to different races," she said. "A race of people comprises all the people, male and female."

Her sincere passion, an intense belief in the truth of her argument, came across strongly to the audience. They listened, spellbound.

"The right to vote cannot be denied on account of race. Neither does sex have anything to do with the right to vote."

She went on, glancing only occasionally at the papers in her hand. In conclusion, she asked the committee to make a recommendation to Congress. The existing laws should be clarified, she said, to include women.

Congressman Riddle rose to announce that Mrs. Woodhull's petition would be closely considered. A report on their decision would be issued as soon as possible. Then the meeting was adjourned.

Committee members crowded around to shake Vicky's hand and offer congratulations. A moment later, she felt herself encircled by many arms warmly grasping and hugging her. It was the feminists, their faces bright with excitement and admiration. The change in them was remarkable. They all talked at once, telling her how brilliant she had been and how grateful they felt.

"The greatest step forward in the history of the women's movement has been made this morning," Isabella Hooker crowed, "and you have made it."

More women from the feminist convention had gathered outside the hearing room, and they, too, fussed over Vicky and her Memorial.

"Please do take lunch with us," pleaded Susan Anthony. "Then we would be so honored if you would attend our convention and repeat your speech for the rest of the ladies."

In a mood of triumph, Vicky and Tennie happily went off to lunch with Susan and her friends. All Vicky's feelings of hurt evaporated. Secretly she had always wanted to be their friend. Now it looked as if she had won them over completely.

Two hours later, she was seated on the convention platform at Lincoln Hall. Glancing around her, she noticed many important people—several senators, the black leader Frederick Douglass, and the officers of the National Woman's Suffrage Association. She tried to smile. The white rose pinned to her dress was beginning to droop.

Susan Anthony, addressing the delegates, described the historic event which had impressed her so much that morning.

"I have persuaded Mrs. Woodhull to deliver her Memorial again this afternoon," she announced. "Although she is inexperienced as a public speaker, she has consented for the sake of the women's movement."

Vicky trembled as she stood at the center of the platform. But once she began to speak, her stage fright disappeared. When she had finished, the hall went wild. Delegates applauded, cheered, and stamped their feet. Vicky had never seen anything like it. Neither, remarked Isabella Hooker, had she.

Fired by enthusiasm, the delegates voted to cancel the rest of the speeches and panel discussions on their agenda. There was no need for further discussion about how women might get the vote. Now, thanks to Vicky, their path was clear.

"It's time for action!" called out one delegate. "I propose we go to the polls and vote!"

Accordingly, a bold resolution was drawn up and approved. It read: "It is the duty of American women to apply for registration to vote. In all cases where they fail to secure it, suits should be instituted."

Small wonder that the captivated feminists adored Vicky. They were convinced that their battle was over.

* * *

Back in New York, the adulation continued. Vicky's new feminist friends called on her at home and invited her to tea. Isabella Beecher Hooker, recently having vowed she would never speak to Vicky, became her most devoted admirer. Often she wrote her letters which began, "My Darling Queen. . . ."

Vicky made headlines across the country. "This is the bravest and best move the women have made yet," one paper gushed.

The Philadelphia *Press* described Vicky's appearance at the feminist convention: "Mrs. Woodhull sat sphinx-like during the convention. General Grant himself might learn a lesson of silence from the pale, sad face of this unflinching woman. She reminds one of the forces of nature behind the storm, or a small splinter of the indestructible."

The weeks ahead were to be the most gratifying of Vicky's life. From all sides came love, admiration, and respect. She received invitations to lecture and soon had embarked on a new career as a speaker. People began calling her "The Woodhull," as if she were a ship or a public monument. For the time being, the public forgot her reputation as a "loose" woman.

So extreme was the praise that a backlash was probably inevitable. One of the first groups to criticize Vicky was the opponents of women's rights. Many people believed the feminists to be a bunch of neurotic women with crazy ideas. The fact that they would associate with a woman like Victoria Woodhull proved it.

The other group that rejected Vicky were the feminists. In those days the women's movement was far from united in its goals. In fact, the women had quarreled so bitterly among themselves that some of the more conservative feminists like Lucy Stone had established a rival organization, the American Woman's Suffrage Association.

The days before the Civil War had been an exciting, romantic time. For the first time in history, a few courageous women began to challenge a way of life millenniums old.

After the war, confusion set in. Some feminists thought

women should concentrate on getting the vote for the Negro. Others, like Elizabeth Cady Stanton, wanted to work for women. She felt unsure about the ballot being the most important issue. In fact, she once said the ballot was a crumb compared to the larger issue of sexual emancipation. The ills of women ran far deeper than merely not being able to vote.

Unlike Elizabeth Stanton and Susan Anthony, many who called themselves feminists did not think family life had to be changed before women could be liberated. They never questioned woman's inferior position in marriage. They were against divorce. They never discussed indiscreet subjects like birth control or sexuality.

In reality, they were like nonfeminist Victorian women, prudish and straitlaced. Lucy Stone, for example, had once attacked the famous actress Sarah Bernhardt and warned people not to attend her performances. Bernhardt, husbandless, had borne four children.

Now, Lucy Stone and others spoke up disapprovingly. They said Vicky would hurt the cause of women's rights. To support her was irresponsible.

Women from the National Woman's Suffrage Association rushed to Vicky's defense. Mrs. Stanton, who had not been able to attend the convention and still had not met Vicky, declared that women should not destroy one another. "If Victoria Woodhull must be crucified," she said, "let men drive the spikes that plait the crown of thorns. This woman stands before us today as an able speaker and writer. Her face, manners and conversation all indicate the triumph of the moral, intellectual and spiritual."

Susan Anthony, traveling in the Midwest, was busy delivering a lecture, "The New Situation," based on the Woodhull Memorial. Wherever she went, she championed Vicky. Those who criticized Vicky got a tart answer. "Mrs. Woodhull's character is just as good as that of most congressmen," Susan snapped. Her tongue could be razor sharp. Once she was debating Horace Greeley, the celebrated New York publisher.

"Miss Anthony," baited Greeley, "the bullet and the ballot go together. If you vote, are you also prepared to fight?"

"Why certainly, Mr. Greeley," Susan answered. "Just as you fought in the Civil War—at the point of a goose quill."

For Vicky, she expressed nothing but encouragement. "Go ahead, bright, glorious, young and strong spirit," she wrote to her, "and believe in the best love and hope and faith of S. B. Anthony."

The House Judiciary Committee rejected Vicky's petition, but this failed to discourage the feminists. Believing she was correct about woman's implied right to vote, they continued to rave about her to anyone who would listen.

Ironically, most women at that time were totally uninterested in voting. They refused to take the women's movement seriously. Even the most prominent women reformers—educated, articulate women—didn't care a fig for the ballot. Two of the women's movement's most formidable opponents were Catherine Beecher and Harriet Beecher Stowe. Both found Vicky appalling.

"She's a snake who should be given a good swat with a shovel," Harriet reportedly remarked.

The Beechers were the most famous, admired family in the land. All but one of the children of Lyman Beecher had distinguished themselves in one way or another. Five became ministers, the most well known being Henry Ward Beecher. Catherine E. Beecher headed the American Woman's Educational Association. Harriet Beecher Stowe, the most beloved novelist of her day, had written a book about the miseries of slavery. More than any other factor, *Uncle Tom's Cabin* had helped to arouse northern sentiment against slavery. And finally there was Isabella Beecher Hooker, a leading figure in the women's movement and the only Beecher who supported Victoria Woodhull.

One of the important points Harriet Beecher Stowe made in *Uncle Tom's Cabin* was that slavery is not only cruel but also destroys the family. The subjects of marriage and the family fascinated her. One reason may have been that her own marriage had turned out badly. Calvin Stowe acted like a typical Victorian husband—he treated his wife like a servant. He was also fussy, tyrannical, and suffered from constipation.

After ten years of marriage, Harriet couldn't stand him any longer. Developing a mysterious paralysis on the right side of her body, she checked into a Vermont clinic for a "water cure." Her husband and three children were left to fend for themselves. Harriet stayed away a year. In the end, she agreed to come home only if her husband promised to treat her better.

Harriet's experience with marriage had not been much happier than Vicky's. It's conceivable that she might have sympathized with a divorcee like Victoria Woodhull. Instead, she despised her and everything she represented. To show her contempt for the aggressive "new woman," Harriet Stowe chose ridicule as her weapon of attack. She began a novel, *My Wife and I,* which ran in monthly installments in the *Christian Union.* One of the main characters was a brazen feminist named Audacia Dangyereyes who sat on men's laps, smoked cigars, and ran around town acting unwomanly. Audacia, a "free lover," was presented as a silly woman with dreadful behavior. Harriet invited her readers to laugh along with her. They did. Everybody knew she was writing about Victoria Woodhull.

Of course, Harriet Stowe didn't know Vicky personally. The serious Vicky could never be called silly or frivolous. If Audacia resembled anyone, it was Tennie.

Harriet's portrait stung Vicky to fury. How dare anyone make fun of her? It was humiliating. And when she felt humiliated, she began to grow bitter and depressed. There were moments now when she'd gaze into the mirror and feel ugly.

"I'm thirty-two," she would tell herself sadly. "I'm old."

Harriet struck at Vicky's touchiest point—she couldn't laugh at herself. To her, life was serious, even tragic, because she had known much pain and suffering. After her appearance before Congress, she hoped the bad times had been left behind. Now she understood that some people would never like or accept her. Respectability seemed forever beyond her grasp.

At this time, when Vicky still smarted from Mrs. Stowe's pen, she first heard the story of how the Reverend Henry Ward Beecher had seduced his best friend's wife.

On the night of July 3, 1870, a frightened and heartsick woman who had been recuperating in the country from an illness returned unexpectedly to her home in Brooklyn Heights. Her name was Elizabeth Tilton, but her friends called her "Lib." She went directly to her bedroom on the second floor where she found her husband, Theodore.

Lib Tilton had come home for the express reason of confessing. She told her husband that for the past year and a half, she had been having a love affair with another man.

At first she had not felt too badly because her lover had assured her their intimacy was pure and holy. Now, overwhelmed by guilt, she could carry the burden of the secret no longer. She spilled out the story to her unsuspecting husband and asked his forgiveness.

Stunned, Theodore listened in disbelief. When she had finished all he said was, "Who, Lib? Who is the man?"

"Promise me you will do no harm to the person?" she begged.

Theodore reluctantly agreed.

The name she finally uttered, in a small quiet voice, was the last one Theodore expected to hear. It was Henry Ward Beecher, the most famous minister in the land.

The Reverend Mr. Beecher had married the Tiltons; ever since, he had treated the young couple like a father or an older brother. He had even arranged for Theodore, a struggling young journalist, to become managing editor of the *Independent*, the country's best-known religious publication. In addition to all this, Theodore Tilton regarded Henry Beecher as his dearest friend.

"Incredible," Tilton thought.

Weeping, his wife implored him to tell nobody what had happened. She wished to blot the affair from her memory, pretend it had never taken place. Theodore, who felt "just blasted," numbly agreed to forgive and forget.

Each of them spent the night alone in separate rooms. The next morning, Theodore went early to his office but found he could not work. Tormented by jealousy, he could think of nothing but his wife's infidelity and his rage toward Beecher.

Lib Tilton had kept her secret for a year and a half. Theodore could not even keep it for a few weeks. One evening in early August he was having dinner with his old friend, Elizabeth Stanton. Before the meal ended, he had blurted out the whole story.

"Oh, that the damned lecherous scoundrel should have defiled my bed and at the same time professed to be my best friend," he cried. "I thought he was a saint. Oh, it is too much!"

Mrs. Stanton thought that she had never seen a person in so much mental agony.

Later that evening, returning home to Brooklyn, Theodore found his wife with another old friend of theirs, Susan Anthony. When the couple began to quarrel viciously, Lib accused her husband of being unfaithful himself. Susan, who had never married, found herself an unwilling spectator to this ugly domestic scene. Finally, promising to stay with Lib for the night, she persuaded the hysterical young woman to go to bed.

Eventually, Liz and Susan, who had been the closest of friends for many years, compared notes on what had happened that shocking evening. The story must go no further, they agreed. It would cause a dreadful scandal.

Earlier, Vicky had heard rumors about the Reverend Mr. Beecher. Once she became friendly with many feminists, women who were also friends of the Tiltons, it was only a matter of time before the full scandal reached her ears. Women like Mrs. Davis and Mrs. Stanton were familiar with the trauma taking place in the unhappy Tilton household. They knew that Theodore had finally accused Beecher of adultery. At first, Beecher denied it; then he admitted his guilt; then he had Theodore fired from his job. Theodore, they felt sure, would retaliate. It frightened them.

The first to reveal what she knew was Pauline Davis. Vicky immediately recalled the mysterious conversation James had overheard the day she made her Memorial speech. What was it? Someone telling Isabella that her brother preached to his mistresses on Sunday mornings. Now the odd remark made sense.

Pauline could not stop talking about Lib Tilton's miseries. Livid, she blamed the situation on Beecher.

"That hypocritical scoundrel" she cried. "Somebody should strip away his mask and show the world what he really is."

"Beecher pretends to be virtuous," Vicky observed. "Even worse, he preaches virtue to others from his pulpit." It was precisely this type of hypocrisy that she had always abhorred.

A few days later Vicky finally met Mrs. Stanton and the Beecher-Tilton story came up again. Liking each other at once, the two women sat in Vicky's drawing room and drank tea and gossiped together like two old friends. Vicky confessed how much she had been hurt by Harriet Beecher Stowe's new novel. Elizabeth Cady Stanton replied that Mrs. Stowe should be the last one to laugh at Vicky when her own brother was a "free lover." One thing led to another until Mrs. Stanton had spilled the beans. Her story sounded essentially the same as Pauline's. Vicky had no doubt that she was hearing the truth.

Shortly afterward, another Beecher entered Vicky's life. She was Catherine, a never-married woman in her sixties and an outspoken foe of the women's movement. Aside from her career as an educator, she had written the country's first popular cookbook. With her sister Harriet, she had also published a book on how to keep house properly. Catherine Beecher had once remarked that since American women did such a miserable job of housekeeping, they certainly couldn't handle a big responsibility like voting. Needless to say, she was dead set against divorce, sexual freedom, and Victoria Woodhull.

Isabella Beecher Hooker could not bear her sister hating a woman she adored. "Just meet Vicky," she pleaded with Catherine, "and you will love her as much as I do." Reluctantly Catherine agreed.

On a glorious spring day in the year 1871, Catherine Beecher arrived at the house on Thirty-eighth Street. "Don't you think the weather is much too lovely to sit indoors?" asked Vicky. "Why don't we go for a drive in Central Park?"

As the carriage rolled along through the budding greenery, Catherine talked and Vicky listened. Soon it occurred to Vicky that this was not a conversation. It was a lecture, a sermon. Catherine's contempt for her was obvious. She behaved like a missionary who has come to convert the heathen from their evil ways.

"Those who insist on attacking marriage and advocating free love," Catherine pronounced loftily, "will destroy civilization. People will behave like animals."

Vicky, who had listened politely out of respect for the older woman, began to protest. But Catherine cut her off.

"If you want the respect of decent people," she clucked, "you must behave like a decent woman."

Vicky could not keep silent another moment. Forgetting caution, she finally said: "Miss Beecher, I'm surprised to hear you condemn me for my beliefs. Your brother Henry is a secret adulterer."

Catherine's mouth fell open. For a minute, the shaken woman stared at Vicky. "My brother has never been false to his marriage vows," she whispered.

Instead of dropping the subject, Vicky recklessly went on to tell about Henry's affair with Lib Tilton.

Catherine gave a strangled cry. "Impossible!"

She looked as though she could kill Vicky. "I will strike you for this, Victoria Woodhull! I will strike you dead!"

"Just don't do it in the dark," Vicky snapped. "I like to see who my enemies are."

Isabella Hooker had imagined that Vicky and her sister would fall into each other's arms. Instead, they parted deadly enemies.

Catherine Beecher aroused Vicky's bitter hatred. She didn't realize how her contempt for Vicky might damage her brother's life. For under Vicky's serene, even temper slept a great hater. She passionately hated class snobbery, injustice, bigotry, and people pretending to be good when they weren't. The Beechers personified all that she hated.

Vicky had become the most talked-about person in the women's movement. When it came time for the National Woman's Suffrage Association to hold its New York convention in May, who could be a more logical person to deliver the keynote address than Victoria Woodhull. A few members complained but to no avail.

The house on Thirty-eighth Street knew an unusual peace. Roxanna, after threatening to leave for months, had finally moved into a nearby hotel. Taking advantage of the quiet at home, Vicky worked on her speech in the library, struggling to analyze her innermost thoughts about equality. While she believed the vote to be an important step forward, she didn't fool herself. It did not hold the key to true equality. Were not the oppressive institutions of marriage and the family major obstacles to emancipation? Wouldn't a sexual revolution be necessary before women could be free?

One thing Vicky understood: Before women could be truly liberated, there must take place a complete transformation in the way society views women. There must be a sort of revolution, but what sort? She pondered this question for weeks.

On the morning of May 11, Vicky mounted the platform at Apollo Hall and surveyed the gathering crowd of feminists. As she began to speak, some of them felt resentment. But soon, caught up in her words, they became mesmerized. Never before had they heard a woman utter such thoughts.

"If the very next Congress refuses women all the legitimate results of citizenship," Vicky was saying, "we shall proceed to call another convention expressly to frame a new constitution and to erect a new government."

"Does she mean what I think she means?" the delegates excitedly whispered to each other.

Flinging out her arms, Vicky answered their question. "We mean treason. We mean secession and on a thousand times grander scale than was that of the South. We are plotting a revolution."

The delegates could hardly suppress their emotions as Vicky thundered on: "We will overthrow this bogus Republic and plant a government of righteousness in its stead!"

Vicky threw down a challenge to her sisters. Not until the female sex revolts, she said, will there be complete equality. By our own actions, we can free ourselves.

Apollo Hall exploded. Women stood in the aisles, weeping and full of rapture.

Overwrought with revolutionary fervor, the convention passed many resolutions before it adjourned. The women demanded reforms in government, education, business, divorce, marriage, and the family. Among the resolutions was one, passed almost unnoticed, which endorsed sexual freedom for women and men. The words "sex" or "love" were not mentioned, of course. But the gist of the resolution spelled out "free love" quite clearly.

Later, when the embarrassed women realized what they had done, they blamed The Woodhull. Who would take them seriously if the movement were associated with "free love"?

The next day the press called Vicky's fiery address, "The Great Secession Speech." Men read about her remarks in astonishment. Their feelings were best summed up by editor Horace Greeley, who wrote in his New York *Tribune:* "This is a spirit to respect, perhaps to fear, certainly not to be laughed at."

Unquestionably, it had been a mad, magnificent speech. But it was not the kind of speech a person makes if she wants to be the next President of the United States.

8

The Unsinkable Woodhull

On April 1, Roxanna Claflin had suddenly announced her intention to change her place of residence. With her daughter Polly's encouragement, she had packed up her clothes and had moved to the Washington Hotel.

At first, Vicky tried to dissuade her, but Roxanna's mind was made up. She insisted that she would not spend another night under the same roof with James Blood.

Vicky was well aware of her mother's irrational hatred of James. She sighed and let her go, promising that she would pay her bills as always.

For weeks, she heard nothing from Roxanna. Ordinarily, the silence would have upset her. At any other time, she would have visited her mother. But those weeks had been busy ones. Her full attention had been focused on writing her secession speech for the convention.

On May 16, while the entire town was still talking about her inflammatory speech, James received a summons to appear in court. Roxanna had filed a suit against him. She charged that James Blood, her son-in-law, had threatened to murder her.

Vicky sensed trouble ahead. How much trouble she never dreamed.

On the morning of the hearing, the entire Claflin family appeared in court. Before the judge could call the proceedings to order, Roxanna dashed up and began to pour out her side of the story. "Judge, my daughters were good daughters and affectionate children till they got in with this Blood. He had threatened my life several times and one night last November he came into the house and said he would not go to bed until he washed his hands in my blood."

The judge banged his gavel, but Roxanna couldn't be switched off that easily.

"I'll tell you what that fellow is," she rattled on. "He is one of those who ain't got no bottoms to their pockets. You can keep stuffin' in all the money in New York but they never get full. If my daughters would just send him a-flyin' as I always tole 'em, I reckon they'd be rich now."

Roxanna's embarrassed attorney dragged her back to a seat. When she finally mounted the witness stand to present her charges, the storm resumed.

"I came here because I want to get my daughters out of this man's clutches," she bleated. "He has taken away Vicky's affection and Tennie's affection from their poor old mother."

Vicky winced. But there was more to come.

"So help me God, judge," said Roxanna, "I say here and I call Heaven to witness"—Roxanna paused for air and then plunged in again—"that there was the worst gang of free lovers in that house on Thirty-eighth Street that ever lived. Stephen Pearl Andrews and Dr. Woodhull and lots more of such trash."

When James took the stand, he patiently denied that he had ever threatened to kill Roxanna.

"One night last fall when she was very troublesome," he explained, "I said if she were not my mother-in-law, I would turn her over my knee and spank her."

Every newspaper in New York had sent a reporter. To be sure, the case was trivial, even absurd. But any information about Victoria Woodhull was considered newsworthy. The press soon realized it would get its money's worth. Their pencils kept flying as one spicy tidbit after another emerged from the testimony.

Before long, the courtroom had turned into a sideshow.

Questions were asked, not about Roxanna's charges against James, but about Vicky and her past. When had she been divorced? Why did she live with two husbands? Vicky and Tennie's unsavory careers as fortune-tellers, a secret until now, came out into the open.

In a desperate effort to get back to the original subject, Vicky took the stand. "Colonel Blood always treated my mother kindly," she testified. "Sometimes, when she became violent, he would utterly ignore her presence."

Tennie, too, rushed to James's defense. Unfortunately, she only made matters worse. She began describing her early life on the road with the traveling medicine show.

"Since I was fourteen years old, I have supported thirty or thirty-five deadheads," she declared, looking in the direction of her mother. "Vicky and Colonel Blood got me away from that life and they are the best friends I have ever had."

Suddenly full of remorse for having called her mother a "deadhead," she leaped from the witness box and, weeping, threw her arms around Roxanna.

"Please, James," whispered the mortified Vicky, "make her stop. She is only making herself conspicuous."

The trial continued for four days until the exasperated judge ordered the case dismissed. But the damage had been done. Woodhull and Claflin's dirty linen had been dumped into New York's lap. Every word of testimony had been promptly reported in the press.

Generally, the skeletons in a political candidate's closet are exposed by enemies. Thanks to her blabbermouthing family, Vicky's private life became the subject of gossip in every household and saloon across the country. In an editorial, the Cleveland *Leader* reminded readers of "the open, shameless effrontery with which she has paraded her name as a candidate for the Presidency." It went on to say that Victoria Woodhull was "a vain, immodest, unsexed woman with whom respectable people should have as little to do as possible."

The press also pointed out, with unbridled glee, that Vicky was a leading figure in the woman's movement.

Feminists who had cheered themselves hoarse for her just a few weeks ago began to squirm, and some wished they had never heard of her.

Refusing to stand by while her presidential aspirations went down the drain, Vicky struck back at her critics. After all, she owned a newspaper, too. In an editorial in the *Weekly,* she tried to defend herself.

"Victoria C. Woodhull's personal and individual private life is something entirely distinct from her public position," she wrote. "Daniel Webster and William Pitt were bon vivants; they were also great statesmen."

And she added, "If Mrs. Woodhull has valuable ideas, what has her past history to do with them?" It was a reasonable question, but nobody was listening to reason.

For the past eighteen months, Woodhull and Claflin's brokerage house had handsomely supported Vicky and her family. It also provided funds to publish the *Weekly.* During that entire period, they were fortunate to have the support and advice of Commodore Vanderbilt. Now, annoyed by the gossip surrounding his proteges, the Commodore withdrew from the picture. Soon afterward, profits began to decline.

Alarmed, Vicky tried to cut her expenses. Servants were dismissed, cheaper food appeared on the dinner table, parties became more infrequent. Soon she was forced to start selling, piece by piece, many of the valuable furnishings she had collected. Her rich velvet carpets were sold. The carved mahogany furniture mysteriously disappeared to pay bills. But the one thing she vowed never to lose was the *Weekly.*

If she had hoped the gossip would blow over, it did not happen. As the attacks on her private life continued, she began to lose her temper. At the end of May, fighting mad, she dashed off a scathing letter to the New York *Times:* "Because I am a woman and because I hold opinions somewhat different from the self-elected orthodoxy which men find their pride in supporting, they have assailed me, vilified me, and endeavored to cover my life with ridicule and dishonor."

She stated frankly that she did not intend to become a

scapegoat or a victim. "My judges preach against 'free love' openly, practice it secretly. For example, I know of one man, a public teacher of eminence who lives in concubinage with the wife of another teacher of almost equal eminence. . . . So be it, but I decline to stand up as the "frightful example!"

The letter closed with a veiled threat: "I shall make it my business to analyze some of these lives and I will take my chance in the matter of libel suits."

Only a few people in New York understood to whom Vicky was referring. But over in Brooklyn, the letter catapulted three persons into hysteria. The one most panicky was the Reverend Henry Beecher.

By throwing down this angry challenge to Beecher and the Tiltons, Vicky unwittingly began to spin a web which would eventually smother her.

Why did she do it? What made her imagine that she could declare war on one of the most admired men in America and win? At this point, it was not her intention to expose Beecher's adultery. She did not seriously plan "to analyze some of these lives," as she threatened in her letter to the *Times*. Libel suits were a luxury she could not afford.

What she did hope for was to silence her critics. Tired of being ridiculed, she fought back in the only way she knew. Her strength, seemingly inexhaustible, had sustained her for many years. Somehow she had survived and managed to reach a position of prominence. She would not be crucified for her beliefs, she promised herself fiercely, not when pious liars like Beecher practiced "free love" on the sly.

In the public mind, Vicky was assumed to be a "free lover." However, she herself had never said so. In fact, as she recently pointed out in the *Weekly,* her private life was distinct from her public position. But she had boldly discussed sex in her newspaper, and she had advocated the principle of sexual freedom on many occasions. This—and the fact that she was a woman—were enough to condemn her in people's eyes.

Ironically, there is no evidence whatsoever to indicate that Vicky practiced "free love." With Canning, she had always been a faithful wife. During the five years she had known James, no other man had attracted her. So far, it had been the idea of sexual freedom that she found so appealing. Now, all that was about to change. Within the next few weeks she would become a "free lover" in practice as well as theory. For she met a man with whom she fell in love.

Late one afternoon in early June, Vicky was sitting in her brokerage office at 44 Broad Street. She was there to check the books and try to figure a way out of the firm's financial slump. Looking up from the ledger, she saw a tall, languid young man with long blond hair. In his hand he clasped a copy of the New York *Times*.

"Mrs. Woodhull?" he began hesitantly. "I'm Theodore Tilton."

Son of a carpenter, poet, journalist, lecturer, intellectual, liberal reformer, feminist sympathizer, Theodore Tilton was now primarily a tormented man. His visit to Vicky's office had not been voluntary. A shaken Henry Beecher had instructed him to see Vicky and shut her up.

Now, embarrassed and clumsy, he handed her the newspaper. "What 'eminent teachers' are you referring to?" he asked coyly.

"I am referring to you and Mr. Beecher," Vicky told him.

She went on to clarify her position. "I certainly do not condemn Dr. Beecher for loving your wife," she explained to the astonished Tilton. "People should be free to follow their natural instincts when it comes to love. But what I deplore is his hypocrisy. Why does he deny and hide his true feelings in this situation?"

Her crisp logic was not what Theodore had expected to hear. Alarmed and confused, he begged her to consider what effect such a confession would have on Dr. Beecher's reputation. And the damage it would wreak on Tilton, his wife and children.

But Vicky continued to argue with him. An hour later, when Theodore departed, nothing had been resolved. They agreed to meet again and discuss the matter further.

A few days later, Theodore invited Vicky to dine with him

and his wife at their home. Lib, a frail, birdlike woman, wore a sad smile throughout the evening. She told Vicky that she taught Sunday school and gave her a book of poems. It was inscribed, "To my friend Victoria C. Woodhull, Elizabeth R. Tilton."

Theodore and Vicky began seeing a great deal of each other. Mutually attracted, they soon became lovers. Theodore's original purpose, persuading Vicky to keep his wife's adultery a secret, seems to have been temporarily forgotten. Now, infatuated with Vicky's loveliness, he could hardly bear to leave her side.

All that summer, the two lovers reveled in each other's company. Sometimes, they would take a picnic basket to Central Park and stretch out in the warm grass. Or they'd go rowing on the Harlem River and watch the sunlight dancing on the water. One afternoon they went bathing at Coney Island, romping and squealing in the icy breakers like two children. At night, Theodore often neglected to catch the ferry back home to Brooklyn. Lying in each other's arms on Vicky's roof, they would sleep under the stars.

James did not object. From the beginning, he had assured Vicky that she was free to love whom she pleased. Now, his beliefs tested, he remained true to his promise.

It is not surprising that Theodore should pour out his marital troubles to Vicky. The irony of the situation was not lost upon her. As she pointed out to him, why did he condemn his wife and Henry Beecher? They had only been enjoying the same good feelings which he now had with her.

Lib Tilton would not have appreciated Vicky's defense of her. A frightened, unhappy woman, Lib was anything but proud of her relationship with Beecher. She believed that she had behaved wrongly, and all that she desired was to wipe the shameful affair from her memory.

"Lib is not your property," Vicky went on to chide Theodore. "You're behaving like a slaveowner."

Intellectually, Tilton agreed with her. But in his heart, the jealousy continued to fester.

The summer days sped by. In his spare time, Theodore

wrote a book about Vicky's life. It was to be used in her campaign for the Presidency. He also wrote highly flattering magazine articles about her, extravagantly calling her "the Joan of Arc of the women's movement" and praising her "moral integrity."

When autumn came, Vicky took to the road. She had little time for Theodore now. Her financial problems had grown pressing, and one way to make money was by lecturing. Fortunately, she received plenty of invitations to speak. James and Stephen offered to work up rough drafts of speeches on topics such as women's rights and sex education for children. Then she would revise, polish, and add her own thoughts.

In those days, listening to lectures and speeches was a popular mode of entertainment. People could learn from them about the important issues of the day. Lecturers had to have something interesting to say, but they also had to present their material in an entertaining manner. Not only was Vicky a great show woman, but she possessed striking beauty as well. Many people came just to gawk. Afterward, they'd tell their friends and neighbors how they had seen The Woodhull in person.

One of her most successful lectures that fall was before the National Association of Spiritualists, who invited her to attend their annual convention in Troy, New York. Spiritualism was a popular but unorthodox religion which had sprung up around 1850 and by now had over four million adherents. They believed that the spirit survives after death and can communicate with the living. A "medium," a person with special psychic powers, is able to receive the messages.

As a group, the Spiritualists tended to be quite liberal in their thinking. Many of them also believed in feminism, communism, and "free love." The Spiritualists and Vicky took to one another at once. Always made to feel ashamed of her psychic abilities and her spiritual guidance from Demosthenes, she was delighted to find a group who believed as she did. At Troy, they unanimously elected her their president. Years later, still overwhelmed by their kindness, she would call the election "the greatest honor of my life."

With most of her time spent away on the lecture circuit, Vicky depended on James and Tennie to operate the brokerage company and the *Weekly*. Every few weeks she would interrupt her tour and return home. On one of these brief visits, she first met Henry Beecher. Theodore had arranged the meeting, the first of many.

That fall, at the age of fifty-eight, Reverend Henry Ward Beecher was at the height of his career. He earned the grand sum in his day of $20,000 a year as pastor of Plymouth Church; its congregation of two thousand was the largest in the entire country. He was so successful that New Yorkers used to say, "If you want to hear Henry Ward Beecher preach, take the ferry to Brooklyn and then follow the crowd." He also earned huge sums of money by lecturing and writing, not to mention paid endorsements for pianos, watches, and trusses.

As a child, he had never owned a single toy because his father disapproved of them. As an adult, Beecher made up for his early deprivation. He bought paintings, horses, precious gems, a townhouse, and a country estate.

His wife, Eunice, lacked his taste for luxury. A cold, jealous woman, she always wore a severe expression. Behind her back, people called her a shrew. Thanks to Eunice, there was little warmth or gaiety in the Beecher household. Back in the days when Theodore and Henry were still friends, Beecher would sometimes lament, "Oh, Theodore, I dread to go back to my own home." Once he admitted the unhappiness of his marriage and told Tilton, "God might strip all other gifts from me if He would only give me a wife like Elizabeth and a home like yours."

Physically, Beecher was a powerfully built man with a ruddy face and a full mouth. His gray hair, worn long, reached the collar of his black jacket. Although not handsome in the classic sense, he exuded a magnetic quality that made men admire him and women adore him. Vicky was later to remark that he had a lot of sex appeal.

Vicky and the Reverend liked each other. Their visits together—which Beecher would later deny—were intellectual sparring matches, each trying to win over the other. Beecher frankly admitted that he agreed with her on the subject of "free love" and divorce. Nonetheless, he said, he could never proclaim those beliefs publicly. It would mean preaching to an empty church.

"My dear Victoria," he teased her in a superior tone, "you are a dangerous radical. Do you realize what happens to militants like you? They are hanged."

"Nobody will ever hang me," Vicky laughed.

In November, the male citizens of New York trooped to the polls to vote in the city elections. Vicky, Tennie, and their feminist friends accompanied them. Carrying a copy of the Constitution, Tennie read aloud the Fourteenth and Fifteenth Amendments to the voting inspectors. Unimpressed, they refused to allow the women to vote.

Back on the road again, Vicky had another clash with Catherine Beecher. Vicky was scheduled to speak in Hartford, Connecticut, on the subject of the Constitution, as respectable a topic as one could wish. Catherine, who lived in Hartford, resolved to prevent the appearance. Writing letters to the local newspapers, she warned the citizens of Hartford against listening to such an indecent woman.

Vicky spoke anyway. Seven hundred persons jammed the Opera House, but if they came for a thrill, they went away disappointed. Her speech, a dramatic summary of her legal arguments on the Fourteenth and Fifteenth Amendments, proved to be a model of learning and good taste. Only at the end did she mention Catherine's campaign to keep her out of Hartford. Turning the other cheek, Vicky said that she hoped "Miss Beecher's conscience will not smite her for speaking so unkindly of me."

In public, Vicky expressed more patience with Catherine than she actually felt. The snobbish, self-righteous woman reminded her of old ghosts—the disapproving women in Homer, the haughty ladies in Canning's family who had spurned her as a new bride, the busybody neighbors in

Chicago who called the police. Curious, she thought, but those who have condemned me most have been women. The thought made her feel more sad than angry.

As time went by, however, her mood grew increasingly impatient. Her fury at people like Catherine Beecher burned at her guts, and she could not rid herself of it. On the other hand, she sincerely believed that most people were decent and fair. What if she were to appeal to their best instincts? What if she rented the biggest hall in New York and frankly explained her beliefs? Surely such a bold move would end the gossip and abuse once and for all. Then she could get on with the real business of her life—campaigning for the Presidency.

On the evening of November 20, a rain and wind storm lashed New York. But there was standing room only at Steinway Hall where every one of the three thousand seats had been sold. One red-haired girl, the press reported, threw off her wet shawl and exclaimed, "By gosh, I hope I haven't come here for nothing in all this rain!" She expressed the mood of the crowd which had not been able to resist the provocative title of Vicky's speech: "The Principles of Social Freedom Involving the Questions of Free Love, Marriage, Divorce, and Prostitution."

A few minutes after eight, Vicky stepped onto the stage in a severe black dress with a pink tea rose at the neck. She was a dramatic, impressive figure as she stood waiting for the audience to quiet down. Gazing at the crowd, she saw that her mother and father were there. At stage left, Utica had engaged a box for her friends. Tennie, James, and Zulu Maud sat in the front row.

She began mildly by going back to the sixteenth century and describing how society had always suppressed the freedom of the individual. Back and forth across the stage she walked, explaining how marriage inhibits personal freedom. "The court holds that if the law solemnly pronounces two married, they are married. The law cannot compel two to love. Two people are sexually united, married by nature, united by God."

Warming up now, her voice began to rise. Her cheeks seemed on fire, so rich was the color of her skin. She continued to attack marriage. Calling it "slavery," she declared that it is better to break up a bad marriage than continue in misery. "All that is good and commendable now existing would continue to exist if all marriage laws were repealed tomorrow!"

A gasp began in the back of Steinway Hall and slowly spread to the front. Amid the hisses was a scattering of applause.

"Any lady or gentleman in the audience who is hissing may come up on the platform with me," she challenged.

Off to the left, a woman stood up in a box. It was Vicky's sister Utica.

"How would you like to come into this world without knowing who your mother or father was?" Utica shouted.

The audience cheered and whooped. Men tossed their hats in the air. "Answer that!" yelled a woman in the balcony, waving her handkerchief.

"There are thousands of noble men and women in the world today who never knew who their fathers were," Vicky fired right back.

Pausing for a moment to wipe her forehead, she began talking about the need for a sexual revolution. Never discussing sex is false modesty, she said. Sex that is not based on love is wrong. One day in the future, "free love" would be accepted as normal and natural.

"Are you a free lover?" she heard someone shout. Finally the dangerous question had been asked in public. Three thousand people looked at her. She saw a sea of upturned faces gazing at her in silence, barely breathing, waiting to hear her answer.

"Yes!" she said in her grandest voice. "Yes. I am a free lover!"

The crowd broke into cheers and hoots. Vicky's voice rang out. "I have an inalienable, constitutional, and natural right to love whom I may, to love as long or as short a period as I can, to change that love every day if I please! And with that right neither you nor any law you can frame have any right to interfere."

Her written speech forgotten, Vicky pleaded with the audience. "I dearly prize the good opinion of my fellow beings," she said plaintively. "I want so much to have you think well of me. It is because I love you all that I tell you my vision of the future."

Stretching out her arms, she explained what she believed in her innermost heart.

"The love that I cannot command is not mine," she said in a hushed voice. "Let me not disturb myself about it, nor attempt to filch it from its rightful owners. Rather let me leave my doors and windows open, intent only on living so nobly that the best cannot fail to be drawn to me by irresistible attraction."

Dropping her hands to her sides, she turned and sailed off the stage.

9

Campaigning

Hark! the herald angels sing,
Glory to the newborn King.

Vicky pressed her forehead against the frosty windowpane and sat motionless as she looked down at the carolers on Twenty-third Street. Tonight was Christmas Eve, but no holiday spirit warmed her heart this year. She was living in a rented room in a boardinghouse on East Twenty-third Street.

Only days after that dreadful calamity at Steinway Hall, the owner of her Murray Hill mansion had requested her to leave. He could not have her kind of woman as a tenant, he had informed her.

Theodore had warned her to expect unpleasant consequences. "It was not your prepared speech which did the damage," he told her. "It was the remarks you made in response to the audience. You said violent things, Vicky. Violent."

Wall Street agreed. For a long time there had been gossip about Mrs. Woodhull. Her customers could—and did—ignore the whispers and innuendoes. They continued to patronize her company because she happened to be an excellent investment counselor. But now that she had publicly proclaimed her shocking beliefs, many felt they could no longer associate with her. They began taking their business elsewhere.

Vicky felt herself on a treadmill to disaster. Her bank account kept dwindling as money poured out to pay bills, especially for the *Weekly*. Little came in, except her lecture fees.

The loss of her splendid house had affected her deeply. Nearly all the fine furnishings had already been sold. But the shell remained—the glittering chandeliers, the gilt cornices, and the silk brocade walls in the dining room. Mourning, she had packed up boxes and valises.

James and Tennie searched for new quarters, a place where the family could live cheaply. The result was this boardinghouse on Twenty-third Street. It was clean, Vicky had to admit, and guests were served plenty of meat and potatoes each night in the dining room. But her days of living like a queen seemed over.

Tonight she couldn't help remembering other Christmases in the house on Thirty-eighth Street. On Christmas Eve her cook would prepare an elaborate feast. The dining room would be garlanded with pine branches, holly, and roses. The table itself was decorated down its great white length with fruit and flowers and tall red tapers.

Vicky's family and friends would sit down to a dinner of many courses: scalloped oysters and Tennessee ham and roast duck with currant sauce, wild rice and beaten biscuits, cantaloupe pickle and spiced cranberries. For dessert, there would be blancmange with brandied apricots, ice cream, nuts, marzipan fruits, and coffee. Iced Roman punch, a heady mixture of rum, champagne and lemon sherbet, flowed freely all evening.

Achingly, she recalled the sounds and smells of Christmas morning, the ooh's and shrieks of the children gathered around the ceiling-high fir tree. Even Byron would be caught up in the excitement. After the gifts had been opened, they would all sit down to a merry, noisy breakfast. Cook would bring out platters loaded with Spanish mackerel, steak, bacon, and fried apples, and buckwheat cakes.

Now it all seemed so long ago. Turning from the window, she said her prayers and went to bed.

* * *

The election year of 1872 was to prove a turbulent one for American politics and for the country's only female candidate. The new year, which Vicky had looked forward to with so little hope, began on an unexpectedly bright note. Once again the feminists were holding their January convention in Washington, the same event at which Vicky had won their admiration a year ago. Despite Vicky's recent troubles, the spirit of sisterhood triumphed after all. Elizabeth Stanton and Susan Anthony, remembering how much they owed Vicky, invited her to address the convention.

When some of the delegates complained, Susan squelched the criticism. Instead, at the convention she went out of her way to pay tribute to Vicky, who sat on the platform in a midnight-blue suit. Susan told the feminists that, on her lecture tours, people repeatedly questioned her about Mrs. Woodhull. Why, they had asked, do you make her your leader?

"I told them," Susan recounted, "that we don't make leaders. They make themselves. If any can accomplish a more brilliant effort than Victoria Woodhull, let him or her go ahead and they will be leaders, too."

Full of affection for the women's movement, Vicky left Washington with an inspired new plan in her mind. Last May, she had boldly challenged the feminists to secede from the union if they were not granted their rights. Since then, of course, no such rights had been granted because no one took the feminists seriously.

"Let them secede," men had chuckled. "They can go to the North Pole and set up a hen state. Good riddance!"

Now Vicky thought of a way to follow up on her secession threat and at the same time promote her campaign for the Presidency. Why didn't the feminists form a political party and nominate their own candidates for office? Naturally she hoped that she would be their candidate for President. When she told this to Elizabeth Stanton, Isabella Hooker, and a new friend, Laura Cuppy Smith, the women reacted enthusiastically. They wrote to Susan Anthony, away on a speaking tour, but she didn't think much of the idea.

"Mrs. Woodhull means to run our ship into her port and none other," she wrote back testily.

Recalling how Susan had defended The Woodhull not a month ago, Elizabeth and the others paid little attention to her reservations. Plans were soon underway for the organization of the People's party. Announcements were sent to the press, and a party nominating convention was scheduled. It was to be held jointly with the New York convention of the National Woman's Suffrage Association in May.

That winter, Vicky concentrated on tooting her own political horn. The *Weekly* provided readers with a running account of her campaign activities, but her chief means of publicizing herself was lecturing. Traveling across the country and back, she shivered in drafty railroad stations, slept in seedy hotels where the bedbugs frolicked at night, and ate uncountable greasy meals.

In Harper's *Weekly,* Thomas Nast, famous for his savage political cartoons, drew a portrait of Vicky with horns and bat wings. It was captioned *Get thee behind me, Mrs. Satan.* Since Nast did nasty caricatures of all politicians, Vicky wasn't too disturbed.

Meanwhile, election fever had gripped the nation's political parties. Right after the Civil War, the Democratic party had fallen apart. It had been the party of the South, although throughout the war there were still Democrats in the North. By 1872, most of the white men in the South and also working-class men in the North voted Democrat. Nevertheless, the Democrats hadn't won a national election since 1856 and would remain out of the White House until 1884. The condition of their party could only be described as a mess.

The powerful Republican party also had its problems. Ulysses S. Grant had been a great general. As President, he had made a lot of mistakes. During his first term in office, there were charges of corruption and graft. Many of his friends made money in ways that were not quite honest, although Americans felt that Grant himself was an honest man.

Unhappy liberals in the Republican party decided to revolt against Grant and form a third party, the Liberal Republicans. A national nominating convention was called to meet in Cincinnati on May 1. The politicians who assembled there hadn't the slightest idea who they wanted as a candidate for President. Finally, on the sixth ballot, they nominated sixty-one-year-old Horace Greeley, editor of the New York *Tribune*. The man who put his name before the convention was none other than Vicky's ex-lover, Theodore Tilton.

The Liberal Republicans almost immediately regretted their action, but there was nothing to be done then. In July, when the Democrats met in Baltimore for their convention, they also endorsed Greeley as their candidate. They figured that if any party was to beat Grant, it must avoid splitting the opposition vote. They were stuck with Greeley, but they didn't like him. They remembered that he had once remarked, "All Democrats may not be rascals, but all rascals are Democrats."

In June the Republicans would convene in Philadelphia and unanimously vote to run President Grant for another term. Thanks to pressure exerted by Susan Anthony and other feminists, the Republicans would write a women's rights plank into their party platform:

"The Republican Party is mindful of its obligations to the loyal women of America for their noble devotion to the cause of freedom; their admission to wider fields of usefulness is received with satisfaction; and the honest demands of any class of citizens for equal rights should be treated with respectful consideration."

This token acknowledgment to "the ladies" meant nothing, of course. In the ninety-six years since the birth of the nation, national elections had come and gone every four years. But they had been exclusively for men. Never had women involved themselves in the electoral process. The year 1872 would be different.

* * *

On the morning of May 9, the National Woman's Suffrage Association convened at Steinway Hall. Susan Anthony and Elizabeth Stanton were barely speaking. In fact, they had spent the last few days quarreling, something they had never done before in their long friendship. Susan had said she would have nothing to do with Vicky or the People's party.

"She is trying to turn the NWSA into a political party for her own ends," cried Susan. "We shall lose everything we have ever fought for." Susan then called Elizabeth "foolish," and Elizabeth called Susan "narrow."

The convention had just gotten underway when Vicky stepped forward and asked the chair for recognition. She wanted to make an announcement concerning the People's party.

Susan, her face pinched, rejected her request. "I have rented this hall to hold a women's rights convention," she declared stonily, "and not for any other purpose. If there is any woman in the audience who is not a member of the National Woman's Suffrage Association, she will please leave."

Vicky, who was not a member, turned and walked out of the hall. Half of the audience, members and nonmembers, got up and left with her.

In the evening, Vicky returned. Entering Steinway Hall by a side door, she ran up on the stage before anyone could stop her and announced that she had hired Apollo Hall. The convention of the People's party would be held there tomorrow.

When a cheer went up from the delegates, Vicky automatically responded. Speaking in a rapid, even tone, she started to tell them that the time for political action had come. If women acted now, they could change the world.

Susan Anthony, her face distorted with rage, rapped her gavel for order. Then she pounded it. And then she shouted to announce the convention was adjourned. Vicky tried to ignore her.

Hurrying from the stage, Susan found the building's

janitor and commanded him to turn off the gaslights in the hall. This desperate tactic worked. Aghast at Susan's hostility, Vicky stood silent in the darkness.

The next morning, six hundred people jammed Apollo Hall. The majority were feminists, but others also turned out: Vicky's radical friends, readers of the *Weekly*, Spiritualists, communists and those who simply came out of curiosity. Their mood was enthusiastic, and their gaiety reflected their sense that this was an historic occasion. Today, May 10, 1872, was the day they would nominate a woman to run for President.

Eleven-year-old Zulu Maud stared around her in wonder. Even though the hall had been rented on short notice, flags were draped on the walls and people carried red, white, and blue banners and signs. The weather had turned warm for May; women had put on thin, summery cotton dresses. Some brought fans to assure a cool breeze if the hall grew too warm. When her mother took a seat on the platform, people clapped and whistled. Zulu Maud had never seen anything like it in her whole life.

The first business on the agenda was to change the name of the party. It was decided that the People's party did not sound descriptive enough. Instead, the convention agreed to adopt the name Equal Rights party. Finally, Vicky was asked to address the session. She rose from her chair and stepped to the center of the platform. The audience was hushed now.

"What is equality?" she asked in her most impassioned voice. "And what is justice? Shall we be slaves to escape revolution? Away with such weak stupidity."

She had to stop after almost every sentence because of the applause. "A revolution shall sweep over the whole country, to purge it of political trickery, despotic assumption, and all industrial injustice."

The crowd roared its approval; someone shouted, "Amen!"

"From this convention will go forth a tide of revolution," Vicky exclaimed. "Who will dare to attempt to unlock the luminous portals of the future with the rusty keys of the past?"

As she sat down, six hundred people stamped their feet and laughed and kissed one another. A judge from Cincinnati rose to nominate Vicky for President. "All those in favor of the nomination, say aye," he cried.

A thunderous chorus of ayes rang through the hall.

The uproar continued for an hour. People marched up and down the aisles, waving flags and shouting "Victoria for President!" Tennie scrambled up on the platform and led the convention in a campaign song she had written, sung to the tune of "Comin' Thru the Rye":

> If you nominate a woman
> In the month of May,
> Dare you face what Mrs. Grundy
> And her set will say?
> How they'll jeer and frown and slander
> Chattering night and day:
> Oh, did you dream of Mrs. Grundy
> In the month of May?

There were many verses, all ending with:

> Yes, Victoria we've selected
> For our chosen head.

People passing on the street and hearing the music came in to find out what was going on. They stayed to sing and march and hear Vicky's acceptance speech.

Tears streaming down her cheeks, she took a deep breath and looked out on the smiling, happy throng. She began by thanking everyone from the bottom of her heart.

"I feel it all the more deeply because I have stood by you so long, sometimes meriting your applause and sometimes encountering your rebuffs. But I have always been faithful to my principles. Without saying more, I again thank you for the great honor you have shown me."

For vice-president, the convention chose black reformer Frederick Douglass. The Equal Rights party ticket would include a representative of the oppressed sex and the oppressed race. Douglass, once a slave, was not present at the convention. He didn't even know of its existence. When he did hear about his nomination, he ignored it and never responded.

That night there was a big celebration. The convention was over. They had broken political tradition; they had done what had never been done before. The challenge had been thrown down to the male voters of America.

The New York *Times*, always critical of Vicky, dismissed the convention in a few words: "Mrs. Woodhull's periodical exhibitions of bitter language attract numbers of idle people."

Smaller papers throughout the country applauded her courage. The Belfast (Ohio) *Weekly Observer* said: "Mrs. Woodhull brings the woman question to the forefront as only an American woman should have the bravery or boldness to do. As long as we are willing to make a woman a queen, we cannot consistently deny her ability to be a president."

A few weeks later, Vicky learned that being a presidential candidate made no difference—if you were a revolutionary and a woman. The landlord of her boardinghouse, perhaps only now aware of her identity, asked her to move out at once. "I won't have no anarchists livin' here," he said.

Once more the search for housing began, only this time Vicky sensed something peculiar going on. At every boardinghouse they met the same answer: "No room." Or, "We're a family establishment."

Next they looked for a house to rent. Real estate agents wouldn't even show her a building. "I don't object to you myself," one agent told Vicky, "but there is just so much prejudice against you in this city that I really can't risk my reputation."

The size of Vicky's family had decreased. In April, after a month's illness, Canning had died of pneumonia. Buck and Roxanna went to live with Polly but that still left James, Tennie, Byron, and Zulu Maud.

"We will have to go to a hotel," Vicky told James gloomily. "I know it will be expensive but what other choice do we have?"

First they tried the Hoffman House in Wall Street where the sisters had first rented space for their brokerage office. The manager, once friendly, politely refused them. So did a dozen other hotels. Finally, they found a shabby place called the Gilsey Hotel where a room clerk accepted their application without a murmur. Unknown to Vicky, the hotel manager was away that day. When he returned and found out the identities of his new guests, he tried to put them out.

Vicky's eyes blazed with anger. "I am a candidate for President of the United States and I am also a citizen," she stated in her most imperious voice. "Unless you can prove I have committed a misdemeanor, I refuse to leave."

The manager slunk away. Next morning, Vicky and James set off for the brokerage office. Tennie went to the *Weekly.* When they returned that evening, Byron and Zulu Maud were seated on the sidewalk next to the luggage. The doors to their rooms had been locked and a guard posted. Undoubtedly Vicky had many friends who would have taken her in, perhaps even found room for all five of them. But she was too proud to reveal her troubles to anyone. That night, and for several weeks afterward, they slept on the floor of the brokerage office. Finally, her sister Polly managed to rent a house for them on East Thirty-fourth Street in her husband's name. Polly had been careful not to mention the name Woodhull.

Just as Vicky was starting to breathe again, a new calamity hit them. The owner of the building at 44 Broad Street raised the rent on their brokerage office by a thousand dollars a year. What's more, he demanded the whole year's rent in advance. She had no choice but to shut down the business, which hadn't been much of a business lately anyway.

Vicky was suspicious. She became convinced that her difficulties could not be accidental. Somebody was deliberately trying to persecute her and drive her from the city. Moreover, she felt positive she knew who was behind it. The Beecher family.

The gossip about Vicky had escalated to a new stage of viciousness. She and Tennie, rumor said, were blackmailing prominent citizens. Supposedly they were demanding huge sums of money by threatening to print scandalous items in the *Weekly*. The rumors made Vicky sick.

She did not feel much better when a woman complained to the newspapers that she had applied for a clerk's job at the *Weekly*, only to be told by Vicky that "we can't have our paper spoiled by women." There were so many lies that Vicky could not fight them all. Besides, at that point the paper was in no position to hire anyone, male or female. On June 28, *Woodhull and Claflin's Weekly* was forced to suspend publication. The money had run out.

"I am paralyzed in strength, health and purse," Vicky wrote to a friend after the *Weekly* closed, "and reduced to a condition in which I am obliged to stop all business."

When her creditors sued her for debts, she testified in court, "I own nothing, not even the clothes on my back."

In September she dragged herself out on the lecture circuit again, weary and discouraged. She went to earn money but also felt a sense of duty. The lectures had been a means of keeping her name before the voting public, but now she could fool herself no longer. Earlier in the summer, the Equal Rights party had organized local political clubs, Victoria Leagues, all over the country. They marched and sang and distributed *Victoria C. Woodhull for President* buttons.

But, as the election drew closer, the Equal Rights party disintegrated. With President Grant rated a shoo-in for a second term, their efforts on behalf of Vicky became nearly nonexistent. Vicky understood that she hadn't a prayer of being elected. Perhaps, in her heart, she had known that fact for some time, but she was not a person who got easily discouraged.

Now she felt herself surrounded by hostility. "Why?" she

would ask herself repeatedly. "What have I done to warrant this abuse?"

One thing she had done, of course, was to thumb her nose at the puritanical codes held precious by Victorian society. The country's sentiment toward her was best summed up by Antoinette Brown Blackwell, a feminist and the first woman minister. Wrote Mrs. Blackwell to a friend shortly after Vicky's "free love" speech: "Independent of the morality of the question, nobody can succeed who begins by so gross a shock to public sentiment."

Another reason for the ostracism: Vicky was a woman. She clearly understood that men, especially powerful men like Henry Beecher, had the freedom to flout society's rules. They could practice "free love" in secret and get away with it. A woman could not. The unfair double standard, against which she had fought for so many years, finally caught up with her. Any woman rash enough to defy the rules that kept women in their place was bound to be punished sooner or later.

All that fall, an obsession gnawed at her. She was seized by a burning sickness to justify her actions and to vindicate herself. Coolly, deliberately, she reached a decision. The printed word would be her weapon. Somehow she would find the money to publish a special edition of the *Weekly* and print the full story about Henry Beecher and Lib Tilton.

And so Vicky prepared a bomb to drop on prudish Victorian America.

10

Freedom of the Press

On the morning of October 28, 1872, Vicky delivered a bundle of five hundred copies of the *Weekly* to a newsstand on the busy corner of Broad and Wall streets.

"Miz Woodhull," protested the news dealer, "I know doggone well I can't sell all these."

Vicky smiled. "Wait and see, Jake," she said mysteriously, "wait and see."

The *Weekly* did not look any different than usual. The front page carried advertisements. There were no sensational headlines on any page. But as Jake began to read the contents, he blew a whistle through his tobacco-stained teeth.

"Good God Almighty!" he swore.

By noon, Jake had sold all his copies. When he ran over to the *Weekly's* new headquarters at 48 Broad Street to pick up another load of papers, he found himself in the middle of a stampede. It looked like every news dealer in the city was there. Finally a policeman was called to direct traffic. Thus the most sensational scandal of the century began with a traffic jam.

This issue of the *Weekly* was no slapdash affair. Vicky, Tennie, James, and Stephen Pearl Andrews had spent over a month carefully planning the detailed expose. The lead article on Beecher, written by Vicky herself, ran eleven columns. She justified her attack on the minister in the name of social revolution. In effect she told her readers that you can't make scrambled eggs without breaking a few eggshells.

If society is to be reformed, a few powerful men like Beecher must be hurt.

"The fault with which I therefore charge him," she wrote, "is not infidelity to the old ideas, but unfaithfulness to the new. I am prone to denounce him as a poltroon, a coward and a sneak for failing to stand shoulder to shoulder with me and others who are endeavoring to hasten a social regeneration which he believes in."

She ended the article with an apology. "I believe in the law of peace, in the right of privacy, in the sanctity of individual relations. It is nobody's business but their own what Mr. Beecher and Mrs. Tilton have done, or may choose at any time to do, as between themselves. And the world needs, too, to be taught just that lesson.

"It is not therefore Mr. Beecher as the individual I pursue, but Mr. Beecher as the representative man, Mr. Beecher as a power in the world. To Mr. Beecher, as the individual citizen, I tender my humble apology, meaning and deeply feeling what I say, for this or any interference with his private life."

Although most of the issue was devoted to various aspects of the Beecher-Tilton affair, Tennie contributed an article about a Wall Street broker named Luther Challis who made a habit of seducing adolescent girls. Her point was that a man could retain his respectable standing in the community, no matter how lecherously he behaved, while a woman could not.

New Yorkers found the *Weekly*'s revelations about Beecher the most horrifying, the most titillating news they had heard in years. Some, never having heard of the paper, asked news dealers for "that paper with the Beecher scandal" and were willing to pay almost anything. The price for a secondhand copy soared from 50 cents to $5 to $10. One man boasted he had paid $40. Those fortunate enough to possess copies rented them out for a dollar a day.

Although people went berserk to read every detail, most did not believe the story. After all, Beecher was a moral leader. Hadn't a publisher just given him $25,000 to write a book on the life of Jesus? If they accepted Beecher as a common adulterer, they might have to admit that their whole moral code was a sham.

Among those who had no doubt about Beecher's guilt was his sister Isabella. When she challenged him to admit his affair with Lib Tilton, he only shook his head sadly and said, "Think how barbarous it is to drag that poor dear child of a woman into this dirt."

Writing to another brother, the Reverend Thomas K. Beecher, about Henry's reply, Isabella said acidly, "So far as I can see, it is he who has dragged the dear child into the dirt—and left her there."

Henry Beecher decided that silence was the best policy. He made no comment, and his congregation at Plymouth Church demanded none. One of his parishioners, stopping him on the street, said, "Of course, Mr. Beecher, the whole thing is a fraud from beginning to end." Beecher looked the man squarely in the eye and replied, "Entirely!"

Outwardly poised, Beecher was consumed by inner turmoil. He sent trusted friends to raid newsstands and buy up all the copies of the *Weekly* they could find. Since Vicky had taken the precaution of printing one hundred thousand copies, Beecher's raids made little difference.

As far as his reputation was concerned, the damage had already been done. Within twenty-four hours, his private life had become the talk of the town and then the talk of the nation.

Around midnight one evening that week, a young man named Anthony Comstock saw a copy of the *Weekly*. His eyes flickered with a positively electric glow. Comstock's mission in life was to track down pornography—or what he considered to be pornography—and make sure that "smut peddlers" were punished.

Until the previous year, Comstock had worked as a clerk in a dry goods store. His crusade had been a personal one, undertaken in his spare time out of sheer joy. Then, in 1872, he persuaded the YMCA to set up a Committee for the Suppression of Vice. Ever since, he had been busily harassing booksellers and confiscating "obscene" literature. When Comstock read Vicky's expose, he could not find anything actually obscene in the language. But, to his mind, the idea of printing such information about a revered minister like Beecher had to be immoral. The next morning he appeared at the district attorney's office and asked them to issue a warrant for the arrest of Victoria C. Woodhull and Tennie C. Claflin.

Waiting for the warrant to be prepared, Comstock suddenly remembered that Congress had recently passed a law making it a misdemeanor to send obscene materials through the mail. Subscribers of the *Weekly* must have received their copies in the mail, Comstock thought. Instead of waiting around for the poky clerks in the district attorney's office, he would ask federal authorities to arrest the sisters.

At one o'clock that afternoon, Vicky and Tennie were riding down Broad Street. At their feet, on the floor of the carriage, lay five hundred copies of the *Weekly* which they were delivering to a newsstand. Their driver, hearing shouts of "halt," pulled over. A carriage drew up next to them, and two men jumped out.

At first, Vicky couldn't understand what was happening. Her heart started to pound.

"United States marshals," the men announced. "Stop in the name of the law."

When Tennie indignantly demanded to know what was going on, one of the marshals announced that they were under arrest. He climbed up on the box next to the driver and grabbed the horse's reins. The other didn't know where to sit. There was no room on the box, nor was there space in the carriage which was stacked with newspapers.

To make certain that Vicky and Tennie wouldn't escape, the bewildered marshal flung himself across their laps. Red-faced, he sat there all the way to the United States Circuit Court.

Tennie burst out laughing and tried to bounce him on her knee. Vicky was ashen but calm during the trip.

At the Federal Building, they were escorted to a private room for a closed examination. Vicky shook her head.

"No," she said. "We want an open hearing because we wish the public to be thoroughly acquainted with this case. Furthermore, we will say nothing until we have an attorney to represent us and until we know what crime we are being charged with."

By this time, a crowd had gathered in the hall of the courthouse. Newspaper reporters, shopkeepers, brokers, and people on the street had congregated to learn what the sisters had done. People stood on one another's shoulders to catch a glimpse of them. "They're both wearing dark blue dresses with purple bows," somebody shouted.

A lawyer was soon found for them, and the group moved into a public courtroom.

Tennie found the experience amusing. "What nonsense!" she declared.

Vicky was not so sure.

Assistant District Attorney Henry E. Davies began by stating the charge. They had been arrested for "circulating through the United States mail an obscene and indecent publication." The offense was punishable by imprisonment and a fine.

Their attorney asked for an adjournment so that he could study the case and consult with his clients.

"Case will be put over until Tuesday, November fifth," the judge announced.

"Your Honor," said their attorney, "November fifth is Election Day. The courts are closed."

The judge corrected himself. "Monday, November fourth."

The assistant district attorney went on to ask for $10,000 bail for each sister, an unusually high figure.

"This is a special case," he declared. "Not only have the defendants circulated an obscene publication through the mails and are guilty of an offense against the law but they are also guilty of a most abominable and unjust charge against one of the purest and best citizens of the United States."

Vicky's attorney hastily reminded the court that the

Reverend Beecher had not charged them with libel. The only charge against his clients was sending obscene materials through the mail.

But the judge could not be swayed. "An example is needed," he said, "and we propose to make one of these women."

He did, however, lower their bail to $8000 each. This made little difference to Vicky and Tennie since they had no money anyway. The marshals took them directly to the Ludlow Street jail.

"This is a monstrosity," Vicky kept repeating to her sister, "a monstrosity begotten by this city's lust, fear, and guilt."

Unlike Vicky, who had sat like a stone during the hearing, Tennie felt no alarm. She tried to comfort her sister by saying they would only have to stay in jail a few days. Besides, it might be a useful experience. When they were released, they could write an article about prison conditions.

That evening, in their new home at Cell 11 of the Ludlow Street jail, Vicky heard more distressing news. Luther Challis, the man Tennie had accused of seducing young girls, had sued them for libel. In his suit he had also named James, who had been arrested and taken to Jefferson Market Prison, a jail popularly known as "the Black Hole of Calcutta."

Both Vicky and Tennie expected that the obscenity charge would be dismissed when they reached court the following Monday. In no way, they told each other, could the *Weekly* ever be called obscene. Despite their confidence, they didn't want to take any chances. Over the weekend, they hired the best lawyer in town, William P. Howe.

Howe, a brilliant attorney, also had a reputation for dressing like a dandy. When he met them in court on Monday afternoon, he was wearing a purple vest, plaid pantaloons, and a blue satin tie. The courtroom was choked with spectators who gaped at Vicky and Tennie as well as the picturesque Howe.

"These ladies are the victims of persecution," Howe said in their behalf. "This case has been instigated by a man who dares not come into court and show his face." He did not refer to Beecher by name, but everyone knew who he meant.

Furthermore, declared Howe, there was not one word in the newspaper that could be called obscene. "If this newspaper is held obscene," he said, waving a copy of the *Weekly* above his head, "then the transmission through the mails of the Holy Bible, the works of Lord Byron, or any edition of the works of Shakespeare should be liable to the same penalty."

To her shock, Vicky learned they would not be given a hearing that day. The government planned to conduct a formal trial. But a date was not mentioned. In the meantime, they were to go back to jail and wait.

Tuesday, November 5, was a momentous day for Susan Anthony. The previous Friday, she and fifteen other women had appeared at a shoemaker's shop on West Street in Rochester, New York, Susan's hometown. The shop was the polling headquarters for the city's Eighth Ward.

"We are here to be enrolled as voters," Susan informed the dumbfounded inspectors.

When told she couldn't register, Susan pulled a copy of the Constitution from her bag. Uneasily, the inspectors finally enrolled the sixteen women.

On Tuesday, Election Day, the same group returned to the shoemaker's shop and cast their ballots, the first time women had ever voted in a federal election.

Susan's vote went to President Ulysses S. Grant.

The next day, surrounded by the latest editions of the New York papers, Vicky sat on her cot and read about the election. President Grant received 3,597,132 votes. Horace Greeley was the choice of 2,834,125.

Some papers mentioned that the Equal Rights party had been on the ballot, but none listed their votes. The election reports gave the impression that Vicky received no votes. As she later learned, this was not true. The Equal Rights party won about 3,000 votes, probably more if one counted the ballots discarded by jeering poll inspectors. When the history of the 1872 election was finally written, Vicky would not even rate a line.

She read the papers wordlessly. For a moment, the months slipped away. Once again she was back in Apollo Hall where six hundred voices were singing, "Yes, Victoria we've selected/For our chosen head." Their thunderous applause had been the sweetest music she had ever heard. She sighed and folded the newspapers.

The days dragged by. Still there was no word about their trial. William Howe was not being very helpful, Vicky thought angrily. All he could tell them was that the government had not yet set a date.

In some ways, jail was not as grim as she had expected. The cells were kept immaculately clean, the meals were generous and not badly cooked. There were even facilities for taking a bath. The warden, overwhelmed by his two famous guests, went out of his way to cater to them. Since he made no objections to visitors, their cell was sometimes packed from morning to night.

Friends, family, and readers of the *Weekly* came to pass the time and cluck about the outrageous way they were being held without a trial. There was noise and frequent laughter. "Cell No. 11," the New York *Mercury* informed its readers, "now well known as the residence of Woodhull and Claflin, was a perfect camp meeting yesterday."

In spite of the "camp meetings," Vicky grew restless and depressed. She couldn't sleep at night. She kept thinking of James in that dungeon at Jefferson Market. She tormented herself with worry about Byron and Zulu Maud, who had gone to live with Roxanna and Polly. Separated from James and her children, she fretted incessantly about when she would return to them.

Zulu Maud, shy and reserved, came to visit her mother. She sat next to her on the cot, eyes brimming with tears, and held her hand tightly. "I have not been a good mother to her," Vicky thought. When she was released, she promised herself, she would spend more time with the girl.

A new worry had begun to trouble her. The *Weekly*

had been closed down. When she was freed, where would she find the money to live? How would she be able to pay William Howe's fee?

Three weeks went by. Then four weeks. She wrote a letter to the New York *Herald*:

"Sick in body, sick in mind, sick at heart, I write these lines to ask if, because I am a woman, I am to have no justice, no fair play, no chance through the press to reach public opinion."

Why, she asked, had they been given no trial? "Is it not astonishing that all Christian law and civilization seem to be scared out of their senses at having two poor women locked up in jail? Suppose, Mr. Editor, that some enemies of yours should throw you into a cell for publishing an article, suppress the *Herald*, arrest your printers, prosecute your publisher, shut up your business office, close all the avenues of press and lecture hall against your honorable defense? Would not every land ring with the outrage?"

When not entertaining guests, Vicky read the newspapers. Horace Greeley, Democratic candidate for the Presidency, died on Thanksgiving Day. On that same day, Susan Anthony and her fifteen friends were arrested and charged with violating a federal law by casting illegal votes. The women pleaded not guilty and each was released under $500 bail. Susan, on principle, refused to pay the bail. Without her knowledge, her attorney paid it for her.

Vicky wrote Susan a letter, congratulating her on the vote and offering her help if it was ever needed. Susan did not reply.

By the end of November, public opinion began to make itself felt. The press, which had originally criticized Vicky for publishing the expose, now said her incarceration was a clear violation of freedom of the press. The Brooklyn *Eagle* said it looked as if the government had locked the jail door and thrown away the key. People began to complain that, no matter what Vicky and Tennie had done, their constitutional right to a speedy trial was being violated.

On December 1, William Howe notified them that two

men had approached him, saying they admired the sisters' courage and would gladly put up their bail money. But freedom did not come so easily. A few minutes after they were released at the Federal Building, a policeman arrested them on a variation of the original charge. On December 5, they were again released from jail and again arrested on still another technicality. But Howe, who had managed to spring James from his prison, kept bailing them out.

By mid-December, it looked as if they might be free at last. The first thing Vicky wanted to do was tell her readers everything that had happened since her arrest. She and Tennie put together another issue of the *Weekly* which appeared a few days before Christmas. But Vicky also needed quick cash, and because she wanted to tell the public her story in person, a lecture was scheduled in Boston. The speech was entitled, "Four Weeks in Ludlow Jail."

The governor of Massachusetts objected violently. "She is no better than a thief or a common streetwalker," he insisted. "I will see that she doesn't open her vile mouth in the city which was so recently honored by Mr. Beecher's presence." He kept his promise.

Instead. Vicky spoke in Springfield, Massachusetts. "They may stop my press," she told her audience, "but never my tongue."

A few days later, she announced that her next speech would take place in New York City at Cooper Union. On January 9, she would tell the full story of the Beecher-Tilton affair, as well as an account of her arrest and imprisonment.

When Anthony Comstock read of her scheduled talk, he got out of a sickbed to pounce again. Under an assumed name, he ordered, by mail, a copy of the controversial issue in which Beecher had been exposed. Unsuspecting, the *Weekly* promptly mailed the issue. Comstock promptly obtained another warrant to arrest them for sending obscene matter through the mails.

On January 9, James was the first to be arrested. Before he was taken away, however, he managed to send a message to Vicky and Tennie, who were at home.

Seizing her cloak, Vicky ran out the back door and took the first ferry to New Jersey. She checked into a hotel in Jersey City under a false name. Tennie also evaded arrest by hiding in a large washtub in the kitchen.

January 9 was one of the coldest days on record. By evening the temperature hovered a few degrees above zero. Howling winds ripped through the streets as New Yorkers found their breath freezing. At Cooper Union, United States marshals guarded the front door.

"No lecture tonight," they told all who arrived. "Mrs. Woodhull is being arrested." About fifty policemen were stationed inside the hall.

Some people left, grumbling. Others stayed and took their seats anyway. Perhaps they remained to thaw out before venturing into the cold again. Perhaps they hoped Vicky would show up after all. Maybe they wondered why so many police were there if Mrs. Woodhull was on her way to jail.

People chatted, rubbed their numb fingers, and stamped their feet to get warm. Among them was an elderly woman in a gray cloak and an old-fashioned bonnet. She hobbled down the aisle and took a seat in the front row. When people began to clap in rhythm and chant "We want The Woodhull," the old woman clapped too.

At last a woman appeared onstage. She was not Victoria Woodhull but Laura Cuppy Smith, Vicky's closest woman friend outside of her family. Announcing that Mrs. Woodhull would not speak tonight, Laura went on to say, "She can't appear or she'll be thrown into jail. Is this a free country? Have we free speech? Have we a free press?"

As Laura was speaking, the audience noticed that the old woman in the quaint bonnet was slowly climbing the steps to the platform. She tottered across the stage and disappeared into the wings. People nudged one another, tittering and pointing.

While Laura was still apologizing for Vicky's absence, the old woman in gray suddenly ran onto the stage and threw off her bonnet and cloak. There stood Victoria Wood-hull, her clothes and hair rumpled, her blue eyes glittering with defiance.

The audience shrieked. "Comstock's been hoaxed!" somebody roared.

Holding out her arms to calm the crowd, Vicky began to speak. For ninety minutes she held the audience spellbound with her story. Not one of the fifty policemen in the hall tried to arrest her.

Then it was over. A marshal immediately mounted the platform and led Vicky away.

11

Hard Times

In 1873 things suddenly began to go wrong for America. Ever since the end of the Civil War, business had boomed, cities had grown larger, people had made money. Now a depression shook the country.

Five thousand businesses failed that year. Banks collapsed; even the great banking firm of Jay Cooke and Company could not honor its financial obligations. Out in the prairie states, farmers had to sell their grain for less than it cost to grow. Textile mills and coal mines closed down. Factories laid off workers or cut their wages.

In big cities like New York and Chicago and Pittsburgh, the hungry and the unemployed stood in long lines to get free bowls of soup and chunks of bread. Desperate people roamed the roads, wandering from city to city in the hope of finding work. By the next year, three million people would be out of a job.

The Panic of '73 hurt many people. Vicky was among them. Although her case still had not been tried, she was out of jail and prayed that the government would find no further excuse to arrest her. She felt a desperate need to put her life in order. After so many nights in jail, after months of never knowing when she might be arrested again, she longed for the comforts of home. In jail, she had looked forward to a normal life: to spending her days at the *Weekly* office like a proper editor and her nights with her family.

She especially wanted to be with Zulu Maud and have long, intimate conversations like other mothers and daughters did. But the peace and normality she craved seemed beyond her reach. She needed money badly. The *Weekly* was coming out regularly now, but its size had been reduced from sixteen to eight pages. Even so, it was costly to print. The paper ate money instead of earning it. Looking for ways to bolster her income and pay the thousands of dollars she owed in legal fees, she ran the following notice in the Weekly:

> The books and speeches of Victoria C. Woodhull and Tennie C. Claflin will hereafter be furnished, postage paid, at the following liberal prices:

The Principles of Government	$3.00
by Victoria C. Woodhull	
Constitutional Equality	2.50
by Tennie C. Claflin	
The Principles of Social Freedom	.25
The Ethics of Sexual Equality	.25

She and Tennie had their photographs taken and offered them to readers at a dollar each.

Still there was never enough money. In February and March Vicky made a whirlwind tour through Massachusetts, Connecticut, Maryland, Pennsylvania, Delaware, and West Virginia. Very often, the turnout was disappointing. People didn't have extra money to spend, not even to hear The Woodhull. Sometimes, glancing at her audiences, Vicky wished for an instant that she could trade places with one of those comfortable wives on the arm of her protective husband. But these were fleeting, guilty thoughts. No, she could never be a submissive housewife, dependent upon the goodwill of a man. She loved her liberty too dearly.

And yet she had to admit that James was less of a husband than she had hoped for. "It's curious," she thought, "but it has been my fate to have had two husbands and neither of them ever supported me." Of course, she quickly reminded herself, James was unique. He had been her teacher, lover, and companion for seven years. No matter what she had decided to do, he encouraged her. No matter what business venture she had started, he pitched in and helped to make it a success. He had even gone to prison for her sake. But he was a follower, content to bask at the edge of her limelight. He had never initiated any project of his own. Never once had she been able to reassure herself by saying, "I can rest for a while—James will take care of the family's needs." Before it had not mattered. Now, for the first time, she began to feel resentment.

In early March 1873, alone in a hotel room in Baltimore, she read a newspaper account of President Grant's inauguration. It had been so cold and windy that his inaugural speech could hardly be heard above the icy gale. The ball that night sounded like a complete fiasco. It was so cold the food froze solid. Hundreds of canaries, brought to decorate the ballroom, had huddled in their cages; some froze to their perches. Guests danced in their wraps, and most went home before midnight.

Vicky believed that Grant had been reelected by corrupt businessmen and rich politicians who had too much to lose without him in the White House. She gazed at Grant's picture on the front page and remarked out loud, "If Jesus Christ had been running against this man, He'd have been defeated."

Yawning, she crawled between the cold sheets. She lay there a long time without sleeping, forcing herself not to think about her smashed presidential dreams. Looking back was too painful. At last, she fell asleep on her stomach, like a child.

Returning home to New York, she felt bitterly tired. Often, in the mornings, she would still be in bed at nine o'clock. Listening through her sleep to the familiar sound of Roxanna's voice coming from the kitchen, she longed to roll over and slip back into oblivion again. Getting out of bed seemed like such a great effort. But get up she always did.

"What on earth's the matter with me?" she would think.

After a cup of tea and a slice of bread, she would feel better and be able to leave for the *Weekly*.

One humid Friday night in June, she and Tennie made a trip to the offices of the New York *Sun*. They paid for an announcement asking why the government had obstructed justice in their case. Why had their trial been postponed for over six months?

Lingering for a while, they stopped to talk to several reporters, old friends of Tennie's. As they left the *Sun*, a heavy rain began to fall, turning the broiling city into a steambath. For some time now, Vicky had been unable to afford a carriage of her own. She and Tennie waited for the streetcar. Riding home, Vicky began to feel faint.

"My chest hurts," she gasped. She could hardly breathe.

"It isn't any wonder—it's stifling in here," Tennie agreed, and began to fan her with a paper. She was worried, though, because Vicky's face looked gray.

Zulu Maud greeted her at the door with a hug. "Supper's on the stove, Mama."

Vicky didn't feel like eating. "I'll go up to bed and maybe have a cup of tea later," she said. She started up the stairs, but when she reached the landing there was a leaden thump.

Tennie and James rushed up the steps to find her sprawled on the floor unconscious. There was no pulse in her wrists and drops of blood were beginning to ooze from her lips.

James stumbled down the stairs and out the front door to find a doctor.

That night and all the next day, the house lay under a deathly silence, except for an occasional piercing shriek from Roxanna. The three doctors attending Vicky concluded that she had ruptured a blood vessel in her lungs. Once she regained consciousness; then, just as quickly, she sank into a coma again. The doctors administered medicines and a mustard plaster for her chest. But they told Tennie and James there was little hope.

The news of her illness had already flashed out across the land by telegraph. Headlines shouted *Mrs. Woodhull Dying!* The press began to compose her obituaries.

"If she dies," declared the Pittsburgh *Leader,* "the world will be rid of one of the most remarkable, albeit terrible and dangerous, women who ever lived in it."

The New York *Sun* said: "If Mrs. Woodhull had been born and educated in a different sphere—if her surroundings had been refined and inspiring—she would have developed into a great and glorious character. As it was, she simply leaped from one excitement to another, wasting her life." All the newspapers speculated on the effect her death would have on the Beecher-Tilton scandal.

Five days later, Vicky rallied from her coma and began to sleep normally. The crisis had passed. Soon she was sitting up in bed, still weak and speaking in a whisper, but on her way to recovery.

As her health gradually returned, so did her worries. At last, the government had set a date for the trial. Months earlier, she had written to her old friend Congressman Butler. What, she had asked, would he recommend as a defense? Butler answered that the obscenity statute was only meant to cover books, pamphlets, and drawings. The law did not refer to newspapers.

This was the line of defense used by Vicky's attorney. On the afternoon of June 26, a wan and thin Vicky sat in the hot courtroom and listened to the jury bring in a verdict of "not guilty." There was no argument and practically no discussion of the obscenity charge. After all those months of anguish, the case was dismissed in a few hours.

Vicky felt that she had touched bottom at last. Surely there was nowhere to go but up. That summer, she spent most of her time in New York. Her younger sister Utica was living with them now. Seeing her every day, Vicky soon noticed something about Utica that had escaped her attention before. She drank—heavily—and her drinking seemed to grow worse with each passing week.

After Vicky's years with Canning, she recognized the signs of alcoholism. There was no mistaking Utica's addiction to the bottle. Sometimes, when she drank to excess, she'd erupt into violence. Once, in a rage, she attacked Margaret Ann with a chair.

At thirty-one, Utica had two unhappy marriages behind her. In her own way she was as beautiful and ambitious as Vicky, but nothing she had ever tried, including marriage, had worked out. Suddenly, one day in July, she collapsed. The Claflins anxiously gathered around Utica's bed, but they did not realize the seriousness of her condition. Utica just lay there with her eyes closed. She felt too ill to talk.

"Oh, my darling sister," Vicky cried, kneeling beside her. "Do you know how much I love you? I would die for you!"

Utica did not reply.

At eleven o'clock that evening Vicky felt she must get out of the house for a while. She began to walk and then remembered she had left a half-written speech at the office. She boarded a streetcar going south. As they passed Trinity Church, she heard Utica's voice. "It's all right now, Vicky."

At the next corner, Vicky leaped off the streetcar and caught another heading back home. Even before she opened the front door, she heard Roxanna weeping hysterically. Utica had died at eleven-thirty.

Roxanna refused to admit that Utica was dead. She kept insisting that her daughter had not been sick. Somebody must have poisoned her. Half-crazed with grief, she could not be convinced otherwise. Vicky and Tennie arranged for an autopsy. The report revealed that Utica had died of Bright's disease, most likely brought on by excessive use of alcohol and other narcotics.

The death of Utica, combined with her own illness, marked a turning point in Vicky's life. She didn't realize it then. Not until years later would she look back, sifting her memories, and see that some secret spring had snapped that summer. Death had touched her. For the first time in her life, she knew what it felt like to be truly afraid.

A year and more passed. One afternoon in October 1874, Vicky huddled beneath the blankets in a Philadelphia hotel room. She was scheduled to speak that night; afterward, a group of friends had planned a banquet in her honor. It was to be a testimonial dinner to recognize the efforts she had made on behalf of her countrywomen. But that morning Vicky had been too weak to get out of bed, and now she could barely speak above a croak. A doctor had been summoned.

Tennie sat on the edge of the bed. "Let me bring you a cup of chocolate and some toast," she offered. Vicky nodded.

Alone now, waiting for the physician to arrive, she wondered how she'd kept going as long as she had. During the past year she had traveled thousands of miles. She had ridden in overheated trains and had made connections in icy railroad stations at all hours of the day and night. In some towns, she had had to scheme and turn on her charm just to rent a hall. When she had secured it, the audience was often hostile. Her previous experiences with lecturing had taught her that such a life was not easy. Still, it was the only way she could earn money.

Wherever she went, she was news. The scarlet woman. The notorious Woodhull. More and more, her audiences were filled with women and young people. After a speech, women would shyly come up to her and say that their husbands had forbade them to hear her. They had come on the sly.

She talked on three subjects: finance, women, and sex. Not surprisingly, the latter was most popular. She remembered giving one of her more radical speeches—"The Scarecrows of Sexual Freedom"—at a camp meeting in Vineland, New Jersey. What a job it had been to get to that godforsaken place! She had taken a train, then a boat, then a carriage —six hours altogether. Hundreds of tents had been thrown up in a field of pines.

At twilight, standing on a creaky wooden platform, her figure silhouetted against a cherry-colored sky, Vicky began to speak. She paced up and down, never taking her eyes from her audience of small-town housewives and their smug husbands.

"Most families are communities of hot little hells," she told them. The women in their calico dresses and the sunburned men in their straw hats winced.

"They say I have come to break up the family," Vicky went on boldly. "I say amen to that with all my heart."

In Chicago, she spoke on healthy sexuality, which she called "The Elixir of Life." As usual, she disregarded what people wanted to hear. She told them what she thought they should know. "It is a fact terrible to contemplate yet it is nevertheless true. Fully one-half of all women seldom or never experience any pleasure whatsoever in the sexual act. I have had hundreds of wives say to me, 'I would not endure these conditions for a single moment, were I not dependent upon my husband for a home.'"

She went on to label wives openly as "sexual slaves." The red-faced women in the audience buzzed angrily.

"Wives may not think they are slaves," Vicky lashed out at them. "Some may not be. But let the large majority attempt to assert their sexual freedom and they will quickly come to the realization."

Up and down the country, from New England to the West Coast, she expanded her views on the barbarous institution of marriage and how it affected women.

"I am conducting a campaign against marriage, with the view of revolutionizing it," she declared fervently. "Those who are called prostitutes are free women sexually, when compared to the slavery of the poor wife."

Sometimes she had to defend herself from angry hecklers. "Prostitute!" a man shouted.

Vicky recoiled. Then she snapped back, "What! A man questioning my virtue!"

On another occasion, after name-calling from the audience, she leaned over the edge of the platform. She bit her lip until the blood came. And when she finally answered, her blue eyes were like steel.

"I am charged with notoriety," she said, "but who among you would accept my notoriety and pay a tithe of its cost to me? I have been driven from my former beautiful home, reduced from affluence to want, my business destroyed, dragged from one jail to the other—all for telling the truth. I have been smeared with the vilest names and called a bawd and a blackmailer. O my God! and the world only thinks me ambitious of notoriety."

With her crimson cheeks and that magical voice which carried to the last row, she appeared robust, a woman in the prime of life with plenty of fire. But her looks were deceptive. Off the lecture platform, she felt tired constantly. She never got enough sleep.

"I feel numb," was the way she explained it to Tennie. Her sister had noticed for herself that Vicky was curiously quiet lately. It was unlike her, thought Tennie.

Often Vicky traveled by herself. Those were the lonely times. For months at a time, she would not see James or her family.

At other times she took the whole household with her. Everyone was put to work. Tennie, acting as an advance agent, would arrive in a town a few days before Vicky, to rent a hall and advertise the lecture. On the night of the talk, James set up a table in the hall and tried to sell copies of Vicky's books and speeches.

Best of all, Vicky had Zulu Maud with her for company. Now thirteen, her shy daughter had reluctantly agreed to take part in the program. Before her mother appeared on stage, Zulu Maud would come out and recite poetry.

Once, Vicky returned to New York to appear in court. The libel suit brought by Luther Challis, the only remaining charge against the *Weekly*, finally came to trial. When the jury brought in a verdict of "not guilty," the judge exploded. "This is the most outrageous verdict ever recorded," he announced. "It is shameful and infamous and I'm ashamed of the jury who rendered it."

Now, beneath the bedclothes in her Philadelphia hotel room, Vicky began to cough weakly. Would the doctor never come? Actually, she thought, it doesn't make much difference. She had consulted other doctors. They all told her she was anemic and left a bottle of tonic beside the bed.

It was difficult not to be sapped of energy when she never got enough sleep, never ate regular meals, and stood for hours. From her hotel window she could see that it was almost dusk. She supposed the lecture that night would have to be canceled. Or perhaps Tennie could speak in her place. The hardships of touring are endurable, Vicky thought, more endurable than other humiliations of the past year. Those who hated her had written vicious pamphlets calling her a prostitute and a nymphomaniac. She felt positive that some of the authors were supporters of the Reverend Beecher. But others, to her dismay, were people who had once admired her.

The most obnoxious pamphlet had been written by a former adviser, Dr. Joseph Treat. Once devoted, he now charged that "you write nothing, not a word." All her books and articles and speeches, he said, were ghostwritten by James or Stephen Pearl Andrews. She was a complete fraud.

Rumors spread until James felt compelled to issue a statement to the press. "I have always found my wife capable of putting her thoughts on paper or before the public on the rostrum much more brilliantly than either myself or anybody else could do it for her."

Being called a fake angered Vicky, but the rest of Treat's pamphlet made her shudder. "Every house she has occupied has been a brothel," Treat wrote. He described how a prominent businessman supposedly said to Vicky, "And what do you charge per night when you are not on the stage?"

"Two hundred fifty dollars," Vicky was supposed to have replied—and then she went with the man to his hotel.

There were many who believed Treat's pamphlet. Vicky considered suing him for libel but she wanted never to see another courtroom again. The law stank; she had no faith in it at all.

The agonizing memories stopped abruptly as Tennie came into the room. Behind her, Vicky saw the doctor. After examining her, he refused her permission to get out of bed.

"In your condition," he warned, "a complete rest is necessary. I advise you to do no more speaking or traveling for at least six months, perhaps longer. Not until you are strong again."

Vicky turned her head to the wall and covered her eyes with her hands. She had never forgotten the bitter hardships during the early days of her marriage to Canning. In recent years she had felt comforted by the knowledge that she could always earn money as a lecturer. Now even that door had slammed shut.

Life weighed heavily upon her shoulders.

Two years had gone by since Vicky had blasted the moral hypocrisy of her age by exposing Henry Beecher. During that time, the Beecher scandal had not died. In fact, it had assumed a life of its own and was quickly escalating to new heights. Even if the nation would have forgotten, Henry Beecher and Theodore Tilton could not. Theodore seemed obsessed by the wrong Beecher had done him. He wrote an account of what had happened. Calling it *True Story*, he carried the manuscript around with him in a leather case and showed it to everyone he met.

The Reverend Beecher's church rose to his defense. It expelled Theodore from church membership for slandering his pastor. Each month some new skirmish occurred in the battle between the two men. Beecher accused Tilton of blackmail, forgery, immorality, and insanity. The congregation at Plymouth Church organized a special committee to investigate Theodore's charges. Lib Tilton, who had left her husband by this time, testified before the committee that she had never had an affair with Beecher. In the end, the investigating committee decided Beecher was not guilty.

All Theodore knew was that his wife had been lured into adultery by Beecher and that now he was being made to look foolish in the eyes of the world. On August 24, 1874, six years after the alleged infidelity had taken place, four years after Lib had confessed, Theodore swore out a complaint against Beecher in Brooklyn City Court. He charged alienation of his wife's affections and criminal libel.

To compensate for his grief, Theodore demanded $100,000 for having "wholly lost the comfort, society and assistance of his said wife."

When the news reached Beecher, he was away in the mountains of New Hampshire nursing his hay fever. He made no comment. Instead, his attorney spoke for him: "Better were it for the inhabitants of this city that every brick and every stone in its buildings were swallowed by an earthquake, or melted by fire, than that its brightest ornament, its most honored name, should sink into deep infamy."

12

*L*etting Go

On January 11, 1875, the Beecher-Tilton trial opened in Brooklyn City Court. It was to continue for six months and provide Victorians with the greatest show of the century. From the beginning, the trial seemed more like a carnival than a judicial proceeding. Each morning, crowds stuffed themselves like sardines into the ferryboats crossing between Manhattan and Brooklyn. They pushed and shoved and fought to get a seat in the courtroom. Some bought black-market tickets for five dollars. Others purchased opera glasses which were for sale in the lobby of the courthouse.

Each day, as many as three thousand were turned away, thereby providing the nearby saloons with booming business. Those who did not get in had a fine time anyway. The area around the courthouse resembled a fairgrounds with refreshment stands and souvenir booths.

Hardly a day went by when Vicky's name was not mentioned in the proceedings. It was she, of course, who had first brought the affair to public attention. But that was not all. The main line of defense used by Beecher's attorneys was that Theodore must be an immoral person himself because of his past relationship with Vicky. If they could prove Tilton had been intimate with Vicky, they thought his whole case would be discredited by that fact alone. It would be an example of the pot calling the kettle black, and in some illogical way, prove Beecher innocent.

Theodore could not deny knowing Vicky. What he did

testify was that he didn't know her very well. His only motive for seeing her had been to keep her quiet. In fact, he said, it was Beecher who had sent him to Vicky in the first place. Otherwise, he wouldn't dream of associating with a woman of her type.

"My association with Mrs. Woodhull was foolish and wrong," he apologized to the court.

Vicky replied with unconcealed scorn in the pages of the *Weekly.* "Mr. Tilton acts like a sniveling little schoolboy," she wrote. "'Beecher made me do it. If it hadn't been for him. I shouldn't have done it.' Mr. Tilton will make quite a man if he ever lives to grow up."

At least one admirer of Vicky's came forward to protest. In an open letter to the New York *Times,* Mrs. Stanton said, "Victoria Woodhull's acquaintance would be refining to any man. In her character and person there is never anything but refinement in word and movement."

When Vicky had first published the scandal two years before, the press had condemned her for lack of taste and delicacy. Now, however, every paper in the country reported each titillating word of testimony. No detail, however trivial, was omitted. And the question everybody kept asking was, "When will Mrs. Woodhull appear on the witness stand?"

She didn't. Both sides were afraid of what she might say. She certainly wouldn't help Beecher's case since she believed him guilty; nor would she aid Tilton, who was busily denying they had been close friends.

She did appear in court once, however. Beecher's lawyers subpoenaed her to deliver any letters in her possession that might relate to the case. Her entrance into the courtroom on May 12 caused one of the biggest stirs since the trial had started. Dressed in a dark blue suit and a black straw hat, she sat with Beecher's attorneys and handed over a packet of letters which Theodore had written her during that idyllic summer. The attorneys read them in silence; then, obviously displeased to find no flaming love letters, they handed them back.

"These won't do, Mrs. Woodhull."

Vicky lost her patience. "Very well, sir," she said severely. "I am not to be the judge of that. But you were very anxious to have them!" She rose and threaded her way out of the crowded courtroom.

Not until June did the case go to the jury. Beecher's attorney summed up the defense's case by insisting that his client, a man whose "silver tongue would lure an angel from paradise," could not possibly have committed adultery. Tilton's attorney declared that Beecher might be a great man but that he was still a sinner. The jury retired.

For eight days, the country waited breathlessly while the jury tried to decide which man was telling the truth. After fifty-two ballots, they returned to the courtroom on July 2 and informed the judge that they had been unable to reach a decision. When the case was dismissed, it was interpreted as a victory for Beecher. The courtroom exploded with cheers and hysterical sobs as people leaped on tables and chairs. On the next Sunday morning, the crowds at Plymouth Church were so great that the police came to keep order on the street.

The trial had run for 112 days. Over two million words had been spoken or entered as evidence. There had been almost a hundred witnesses. It would go down in history as one of the most discussed trials in American jurisprudence.

Beecher's triumph could not help but add to Vicky's bitterness. She had suffered by practicing what she sincerely believed. Henry Beecher practiced what she believed, too, but he did not suffer. As far as she was concerned, he had lied his way through the trial—nine hundred times he had said, "I don't know," or, "I can't recollect"—but still the nation crowned him as its idol. In a twisted way, she drew a lesson from the Beecher-Tilton trial: dishonesty can be the best policy.

Vicky began the Beecher drama. By the time it had been played to its deceitful end, it destroyed her psychologically. She was no longer the same woman; in fact, she would never be that person again. Justice had not triumphed. Instead, it had risen and strangled her.

Vicky dozed against the coach seat on a train between Chicago and Milwaukee and clung to her mother's leathery hand. Trees flashed by the window and, when she half-opened her eyes, she could catch a glimpse of Lake Michigan.

"I won't stand to rest till I get you to that hotel and into bed," Roxanna was saying. "Looks like you're wore out, darlin'."

From a satchel at her feet, Roxanna pulled out a chunk of cornbread and an orange. "I reckon we got quite a piece to go yet. Better take something to eat, darlin'."

"Yes, Mama," said Vicky, hunched against her mother's shoulder.

There was no more fight left in her. Sometimes she thought that touring the lecture circuit was like living in a dream. Memphis, Dallas, Binghamton, St. Louis—all cities looked alike to her. She grieved to herself that her health was ruined and her appearance wretched. If pleurisy or anemia didn't plague her, then pains in her chest and shortness of breath did.

Her life had become a series of melodramas. At each new town, she'd unpack and try to pull herself together. She would get buttoned into one of her stylish dresses and pin her trademark, a fresh rosebud, at her throat. Before leaving for the lecture hall, she'd swallow a cup of scalding tea with plenty of honey. If she were having one of her really bad days, she'd lace the tea with a spoonful of brandy.

In command of herself then, she would be able to walk confidently onto the stage and speak for an hour and a half, sometimes two hours. Immediately afterward, she would collapse.

The one person who kept her going was Roxanna. It was Roxanna who insisted she accompany Vicky on tour, Roxanna who packed and unpacked, argued with hotel porters, put Vicky to bed at night and dragged her out of bed in the morning. She dressed Vicky and fed her and gave her medicine. She fussed over her daughter as she had never done when Vicky was a child.

Vicky didn't object to Roxanna's babying. The truth was she felt like a helpless child. She desperately wanted to be mothered and taken care of. Traveling with Roxanna, Tennie, and Zulu Maud was curiously comforting. It reminded her of the old days when the Claflin medicine show roamed the Midwest, telling fortunes and promising astounding cures.

Roxanna, now in her seventies, was a powerful old woman with strong shoulders and an active tongue. In fact, she never stopped talking. Vicky let her prattle on, thankful for her comforting presence. Roxanna's favorite opening phrase was, "I just used to set there and keep my mouth shut. . . ." Then she'd go on to tell Vicky what she thought of her radical ideas on feminism, politics, and sex. All her tirades ended on the same note: "Well, I knowed doggone well it were the work of the devil."

While Roxanna talked, Vicky listened. It would be too easy to suggest that Roxanna was responsible for the changes taking place in Vicky. Roxanna was only one influence among many; she only hastened the final outcome. But there was no doubt that a new Victoria Woodhull now appeared on the lecture platform.

Gradually she spoke less and less about sexual freedom and the slavery of marriage. She began to talk more about God and religion. A statue of the Virgin Mary began to appear on the platform with her. She'd begin a lecture by opening a morocco-bound Bible and reading from the Scriptures. She composed new speeches and called them "The Human Body, the Temple of God" and "The Garden of Eden, or Paradise Lost and Found."

The latter dealt with menstruation, which proved the old, bold Vicky had not vanished entirely. In those days, menstruation was a taboo subject. Nobody, man or woman, discussed woman's "curse" in public. But Vicky's radical statements grew less frequent, both on the lecture platform and in the pages of the *Weekly*.

Some people welcomed her new image. One newspaper noted that her lectures "could be heard without shame by every woman, man and child in the city."

Nevertheless, readers of the *Weekly* were puzzled at this new turn of events. They wanted to read about social revolution, not religion. "Has Mrs. Woodhull gone over to the Roman Catholic Church?" demanded one irate subscriber. Some readers canceled their subscriptions, others simply never renewed them. James, who had been left behind in New York to work on the paper, saw what was happening and tried to warn Vicky. Closing her eyes, she continued to send him articles on the meaning of the book of Genesis and the Revelations of Saint John the Divine.

On June 10, 1876, *Woodhull and Claflin's Weekly* was forced to suspend publication. With the exception of six months in 1872, when Vicky had gone broke and then to jail, the *Weekly* had run for over six years. By this time, practically nobody remembered its original purpose: to promote Victoria Woodhull for President.

In the final issue Vicky fervently denied that she had ever supported "free love." She insisted that she had always advocated "the sanctity of marriage."

"Nor do I believe," she added, "in the loose system of divorces now so much in vogue. To me, this business is as reprehensible as the promiscuousness that runs riot in the land."

She had lived hard, but now her body and spirit failed her. Unlike other despondent women, she disdained ordinary methods of escape such as alcohol, drugs, or suicide. Instead, unconsciously perhaps, she destroyed herself in a far more dramatic way. She systematically denied all she had ever been.

Almost viciously, she slashed her ties with everything she had once held dear. Some said she had been a fake all along. Others found her actions a mystery. But there really was no mystery. And it wasn't a matter of suddenly abandoning her beliefs in sexual freedom or divorce or women's rights. The truth was, she didn't believe in anything anymore.

Despite her new defense of marriage, she no longer believed in it either. At least not with James. She no longer loved him. For that matter, the very thought of him infuriated her. He didn't know how to make money and he could not offer her the emotional security she needed.

While seriously ill, she had practically crawled from city to city just to earn money for them. James, sitting comfortably in New York, wrote a few articles each week and waited for her to mail him money. It was intolerable, she fumed. Month after month in her mother's company only reinforced her rage. Roxanna had always hated James. She talked endlessly and obsessively about his shortcomings as a husband.

During their entire marriage, James had never earned money to support Vicky. Quite the opposite. He had allowed Vicky to support him. Was that manly, Roxanna demanded? Was it right for Vicky to work and slave while James sat in New York like a prince?

Sometimes Vicky tried not to listen to Roxanna, but eventually she was forced to agree. In the fall of 1876, without emotion or regret, she sued James for divorce. She had divorced him once before, shortly after their marriage, to prove their love would be free. By now, however, the law apparently recognized her as a common-law wife since they had lived together for ten years. This divorce marked the end of their once-loving friendship.

Abandoning her past was one thing; burying it proved far more difficult. She wanted a new life, but people had good memories. Everywhere she went, there were constant reminders. Every newspaper had a library full of clippings to document what she had once said.

Slowly a plan began to take shape within her tired mind. It was the old Claflin cure for trouble. Moving. Going someplace new where nobody knows you. Except this time, where could she move? It would have to be someplace far away.

In August 1877 Vicky sailed for England. With her went Roxanna and Buck, Tennie, Byron, and Zulu Maud. There was nothing left for her in America, she thought. Perhaps life in England would be better. She would lecture. She might even start another newspaper. Maybe she could find a cottage with a garden in some quiet, restful village. She didn't know. But, for better or worse, she had made her decision.

Her departure did not pass unnoticed. In fact, a fresh batch of rumors started to circulate immediately. Earlier in the year, Commodore Vanderbilt had died. He left a fortune of over $100 million, most of which he willed to his son William. His other children, determined to break the will, said that their father had not been in his right mind for years. To prove his eccentricity, they pointed to his association with Victoria Woodhull and Tennie Claflin.

People said that William Vanderbilt feared the sisters might be called as witnesses in the trial to contest the Commodore's will. They said he paid them a handsome sum of money to leave the country for a while. People wondered how Vicky, recently so penniless, could suddenly uproot and move her whole family to England. Vicky, however, always denied that she had been paid off.

"William H. Vanderbilt had no more to do with my departure than did the youngest child in San Francisco," she stated flatly.

In England she felt as if her life were starting all over again. After a two-month rest, her health improved and some of her old energy returned. The violet circles around her eyes began to fade.

Already she had made inquiries about appearing in English lecture halls. Now Tennie acted as her manager by going around with a scrapbook full of newspaper clippings to show that Vicky was a well-known speaker in America. Only the complimentary reviews were selected; any which smacked of notoriety was discarded.

Vicky made her debut in the provinces, first in Nottingham, then in Liverpool and Manchester. From the radical title of her speech, "The Human Body, the Temple of God," her audiences expected to be shocked. What they got was a conservative lecture on physical hygiene and religion. She advised English mothers to inform their children about sex.

Although one newspaper said that "no man would dare discuss such subjects as Mrs. Woodhull is ready to discuss anywhere," her notices were generally favorable. "Mrs. Woodhull is unquestionably a great orator," reported the Nottingham *Guardian,* "and it is not difficult to understand how she has gained so remarkable a hold upon the people of her own country."

In many ways, Vicky felt at home with the English. They were a gracious, cheerful people, she decided; but English high society appeared much too snobbish to suit her taste. They didn't respect anyone except those of their own class and position. It seemed to Vicky that they were obsessed with what is "respectable" and what isn't. She quickly discovered that a divorced woman isn't. Since she had little contact with the upper class, however, none of this disturbed her.

Shortly before Christmas, Vicky was scheduled to speak at St. James's Hall in London. Prior to the lecture, she managed to capture some publicity for herself. Announcements were sent to the press, and as a result, several papers interviewed her. To her dismay, she found that the papers investigated her background more thoroughly than she expected. Her connection with "free love" was mentioned, as well as the rumors about her supposed involvement with William Vanderbilt in the contested will case.

Despite these unpleasant moments, she felt a sense of joy about her new life. How thankful she was to feel well again. How thrilling to be speaking in a famous hall like St. James's! In fact, the entire city of London delighted her. It was the biggest place she had ever seen. There were rows of little houses, all looking very much alike, next to great mansions and palaces. She loved the labyrinth of streets, some narrow and winding, others wide promenades, and she delighted in the lush green parks punctuated by soaring church spires.

On the evening of her lecture at St. James's, she had never looked more ravishing. Dressed in an elegant black silk dress trimmed with bands of velvet, a pink rose with a geranium leaf at her neck, she looked like the old buoyant Vicky. During her first moments on the platform, she shivered from uncustomary nerves. But soon her eloquence returned. The excitement she felt at being there must have been contagious because, afterward, there were waves of applause.

Among the enthusiastic crowd, in a box near the platform, sat a strikingly handsome man with a beard and big childish eyes. He wore a frock coat and white kid gloves, and he clapped harder than anyone. John Martin, a banker, was thirty-six but looked younger than his age. His wealthy, aristocratic family owned Martin's Bank, an institution that dated back to the time of King Edward IV. It was older than the Bank of England.

Throughout the lecture, John Martin stared at Vicky through opera glasses. Occasionally, he'd pass the glasses to the friend who had accompanied him. Martin remarked, "I am charmed by her high intellect and fascinated by her manner."

His friend commented that Vicky was not entirely respectable.

John Martin made no reply. When the applause had died and Vicky had left the stage, he hurried backstage to pay his respects.

Vicky, her eyes still blazing with excitement, was surrounded by a crowd of admiring well-wishers. When John Martin came up to congratulate her, she noticed only that he was eager and very attractive.

"May I have the pleasure of calling on you someday soon?" he asked politely.

"Certainly," she answered. As he left, he pressed an engraved card into her hand. Later, after nearly everyone had departed, she looked at the card. The name read John Biddulph Martin, Esq. When she asked a woman standing nearby who the young man was, she was told that Martin happened to be the most eligible bachelor in England.

Vicky could not have known John Martin's enthralled mood as he left the lecture hall. "If Mrs. Woodhull would marry me," he confided to his friend, "I would certainly make her my wife."

But perhaps her power of extrasensory perception was working that night, after all. For she felt hopelessly gay.

When she left St. James's Hall, snow was falling gently. Halfway back to her lodgings, she asked the cabman to stop. Stepping out, she stood there dreamily for a moment and let the velvet flakes melt on her cheeks.

Over the next few months, Vicky saw a great deal of John Martin. They dined on lobster salad and champagne at London's most fashionable restaurants. At Covent Garden, they were seen attending the opera. When spring arrived, they rode every afternoon along the gravel paths of Kensington Gardens.

She found him kind, considerate, and almost fatherly despite the fact that he was three years her junior. From the beginning, one fact was clear. John adored her. He made no secret of his infatuation.

The night he formally proposed, she burst into tears. If she didn't love him before, she did then. More than anything else in the world, she wanted someone to protect her. Never again did she want to worry about money or contemptuous people calling her names. By marrying John, a completely new life would be possible.

That very first time they had met, John had declared that if she would marry him, he wanted her. Vicky was willing, but the Martin family was not. John's doting mother frowned upon her son's association with Vicky. She called her "an adventuress." When Mrs. Martin heard that John wanted to marry Vicky, she was appalled.

"A divorced woman!" she exclaimed. "A woman divorced twice!"

As time went by, Mrs. Martin became even more resistant. The longer Vicky remained in England, the more sensational information about her past was dug up by the press. Soon London's most fashionable drawing rooms began to buzz with unsavory gossip.

"That woman," Mrs. Martin firmly told her son, "is not the sort of woman a man marries."

Fortunately for Vicky, John did not believe the gossip. Rarely did he question her in any detail about her past. Whatever she told him, he accepted because he loved her.

Still, he would not defy his mother's wishes; he refused to marry Vicky unless his family consented.

Frantic at the prospect of losing John, Vicky embarked on a remarkable campaign of denial. Except for women's rights, she disavowed nearly everything she had ever said or done. Vicky knew what she wanted. To get it, she was willing to lie.

"I'm nearly forty," she cried to Tennie. "This is my last chance."

In the end, she did marry John Martin. But it took her six long years to become what she once despised: a "respectable" married lady.

13

End of the Dream

The first winter of her marriage, she went to live at 17 Hyde Park Gate, the sumptuous Martin mansion with its blue-and-gold-ceilinged entranceway and its marble busts of Aphrodite and Hermes. In the drawing room, the parquet floors had been covered with bearskin rugs, and a Venetian wood chandelier was carved with little cupids. Most stunning was a silver statue of the goddess Nike against a background of black velvet.

Despite its grandeur, Vicky found the mansion cold and lonely. None of John's snobbish friends visited her. Once her husband's club gave a dinner to which wives were invited. When John invited her and Tennie, the other wives boycotted the affair, saying they couldn't associate with them. In the end, she and Tennie had been the only women present at the dinner.

Two years after Vicky had finally wed John Martin, Tennie married an elderly widower, Sir Francis Cook. The owner of an importing firm, Cook was even wealthier than Vicky's husband. He lived in a magnificent home on the Thames River, Doughty House. He also owned a large estate in Portugal where the king had granted him the title of Viscount de Montserrat.

Despite Vicky and Tennie's high position, people continued to snub them. Tennie didn't seem to mind, but Vicky felt humiliated and constantly struggled so that John would not regret having married her. Yet her past haunted their marriage. People insisted on talking and writing about her—the Beecher scandal, "free love," her many husbands, her career as a fortune-teller.

During the 1880s and '90s, she crossed the ocean countless times to answer her American critics in person. It never did a bit of good. Each time she appeared in her native country, there would be a fresh wave of sensational stories in the papers. Tennie said it was because she was rich now, and people enjoyed persecuting the rich. Perhaps, but she could never ignore an attack. Each time, she'd book passage and sail back to do battle.

There were other trips, too. Several times she returned expressly to renew her campaign for President. These were merely gestures; futile ones, she had to admit. Mostly, she wanted to impress John's family and to show English society that she was an important person. But the English continued to ignore her, and the Americans laughed. A Chicago paper described her as a middle-aged woman with the sharp, eager look of an adventuress.

In 1892 John rented a house in New York while Vicky tried to muster political support as a feminist candidate for President. Collecting fifty women, she formed the Humanitarian party to run her against Grover Cleveland. At once, she received a hailstorm of indignant protests from the feminists. How dare she, a foreigner, presume to speak for American women! Lucy Stone claimed that not one of the women supporting Vicky was a bona fide feminist. Frances Willard, speaking for the National Woman's Suffrage Association, warned that Vicky could run for President if she wanted, but she shouldn't link her name with such saints as Susan Anthony.

The following year she returned to America for a lecture tour. In New York she spoke at Carnegie Hall on "The Scientific Propagation of the Human Race." A big crowd turned out to witness her comeback after seventeen years away from the lecture platform. She was dressed in violet with a bunch of violets at her throat. But people went away disappointed because she had lost her fire and fizz. Then in her mid-fifties, she wore glasses to read her speech. The evening fell flat; upset, she canceled the rest of her tour. The years before the turn of the century were stormy. One of Vicky's biggest troubles was learning to live with boredom. Much of her restless traveling across the Atlantic and her weak attempts at politics resulted from having nothing to do. As much as she loved her husband, the monotonous life of a wealthy English matron bored her to death, and she came to regard the Martin mansion as a mausoleum. Time hung heavily on her hands.

Once, searching for distraction, she decided to write her autobiography. At a rosewood writing desk before a fire in her bedroom, she began:

"Sitting here today in this north room of 17 Hyde Park Gate, London—dreary, smoky, foggy, insulated as you are in the customs and prejudices of centuries—I am thinking with all the bitterness of my woman's nature how my life has been warped and twisted out of shape by this environment, until, as I catch a glimpse of my haggard face in the mirror opposite, I wonder whether I shall be able to pen the history of this stormy existence."

As it turned out, she was not able to pen her history. She gave up after writing a dozen pages. Many of the memories that pleased her she had already denied; the rest were too sad to dwell upon. An autobiography should tell the truth. She couldn't.

Besides, she knew that her story was badly written as well as bitter. Better that she stick to an impersonal medium like journalism. In the 1890s she launched a new journal, the *Humanitarian*. Instead of choosing Tennie as her associate, this time she selected her daughter. Zulu Maud had none of her mother's dashing qualities. Sweet and gentle, she seemed content to devote her life to Vicky. In truth, Vicky discouraged her from marrying, but Zulu did not appear to care. For a half dozen years, Zulu helped her edit the *Humanitarian*. It was a handsome publication which looked like *Woodhull and Claflin's Weekly*. But the resemblance ended there. The new journal dealt mildly with social themes but lacked the fire that had made the *Weekly* so memorable.

After John Martin's death in 1897, Vicky made no more trips to America. Closing down the *Humanitarian* and the house at 17 Hyde Park Gate, she took the $850,000 he left her and, with Byron and Zulu Maud, moved to Norton Park, the Martin family estate in Worcestershire. It was hers now.

All her life, happiness had been hard to find; in truth, it had always eluded her. The closest she came to peace were her years at Norton Park. There, on a small scale, she lived the life of a queen, or a president. Her constituency was the ancient village of Bredon's Norton. She repaired its roads, renovated its quaint thatched cottages, and installed electric street lighting. She educated the local farmers about new methods of agriculture. One year, she divided up a farm she owned and rented the land to women so that they might learn to farm.

After hearing about a new method of education for very young children—the kindergarten system—she built a school on her estate, hired trained kindergarten teachers, and provided bus service so that children from the surrounding villages could attend.

Demosthenes had prophesied that she would lead her people; there, in Bredon's Norton, she tried. She established an annual flower show which, as years passed, became the largest agricultural fair in that section of England. She also brought culture to the village. Renovating an old barn on her property, she turned it into a hall where she arranged lectures, pageants, and Christmas parties with carols sung by the village choir.

On a foggy January afternoon in 1923, Vicky sat impatiently in the rear seat of her shiny white limousine. It seemed as if they had left London hours ago and still they were nowhere near Norton Park.

She fought an urge to yell at her chauffeur. His driving annoyed her. In good weather she had to remind him constantly to drive faster. She loved cars; in fact, she had been one of the first in England to own one. But she also enjoyed speeding.

That day there was no use insisting the chauffeur speed up. The fog grew worse than ever. Blurred shapes of trees and houses surged slowly by the window. Now and then she could see an electric light glowing dimly in the thick grayness. It was almost as dark as night.

From head to toe, Vicky was enveloped in fur. A dark fur hat covered her white hair; over the lap of her sable coat, a fur rug was thrown. All that showed were her fragile face, still as exquisite as a cameo, and her thin hands crisscrossed by blue veins. She turned to Zulu Maud with a sigh and asked the time.

Her daughter told her that it was almost four.

Then she fell silent again, trying hard to clear her mind of all thoughts. But the painful emotions kept hammering their way to the surface. "Why did Tennie have to go and die!" she cried to herself. Tennie dead! When the telegram had arrived the week before, she had refused to believe it. "She couldn't be dead," she'd moaned to Zulu. "She's only seventy-seven!" She had always imagined Tennie, seven years her junior, would outlive her.

Eighty-four! She hadn't felt her age, at least not until the past week. Now she suddenly realized that everyone but her had passed away—Roxanna and Buck and her sisters and brothers. All three of her husbands were dead: John, who succumbed to pneumonia in the eighteenth year of their marriage; James, who went to hunt gold in Africa and died there of a fever; Canning, released these many years from the grip of alcohol and morphine.

Even those whose paths she had crossed briefly were no longer living. The feminists came to mind—Susan Anthony, Elizabeth Stanton, Lucy Stone, Isabella and Pauline. For the first time in years, she thought of Henry Ward Beecher. After he died of a stroke in 1887, the mayor of Brooklyn declared a public holiday. Fifty thousand persons, mostly women, lined the streets to watch his funeral procession. Poor Lib Tilton survived him by another ten years. When she publicly confessed that Beecher had been her lover after all, the minister declared she was unbalanced and never spoke to her again. She went to live with one of her daughters and became a recluse. When Lib died, she was buried in the same cemetery as Beecher.

And Theodore Tilton. Vicky remembered that, after the trial, he traveled around the country lecturing. Finally he went to Paris where he wrote poetry and played chess until he died in 1907.

Driving up to London for Tennie's funeral had stirred a thousand memories in her. Since she'd given up her London home and retired to the country twenty years before, she and Tennie had been less close. Tennie never changed, though. Whenever she visited Vicky, she'd curl up in a chair reading trashy mystery novels. She wore ruffled frocks too youthful for her age and, in Vicky's opinion, too much makeup. During the war, she'd talked about organizing women into an amazon army, but nothing ever came of it.

The car came to a stop at a village crossroads. Staring out into the blackness, she could see shrouded figures come into view and then vanish. This fog will last until spring, she thought wearily. She had grown to hate the uncomfortable English winters with their smog and drizzle and snow. Suddenly she remembered to ask Zulu Maud about Tennie's obituaries. The *Times,* her daughter said, had called her Tennessee Claflin instead of Lady Cook. The obituary mentioned that Tennie had been a pioneer in the women's rights movement and that she had studied law, banking, and medicine.

Hearing the latter, Vicky must have smiled into her furs. What would the papers say about her when she died? Would they forget her tempestuous past, as they had Tennie's?

As the car left the Avon River and turned up the winding graveled road to her home, Vicky stirred restlessly under her furs. Still half lost in reverie, she passed her orchards, the park of evergreens, and then the manor house which had been built before Shakespeare's time. The smaller of two dwellings on her estate, it was a wonderful old place with hidden cupboards in the oak paneling and even a secret passage.

The car crossed a bridge over a foamy stream and drew up in front of Norton Park, the estate's main house. In summer its gables were overgrown with ivy and roses, but now the massive house loomed dark and ominous in the swirling fog. Vicky felt empty and depressed.

That summer she went to Brighton, the popular seaside resort, in the hope that the ocean air might restore her vitality. Low in spirits after Tennie's death, she also began to suffer from heart trouble.

Zulu Maud noticed that her mother was growing increasingly eccentric. Vicky demanded that all the windows in the house be heavily curtained. She allowed no doors to be closed in any room she happened to be occupying. She also avoided shaking hands with people because she feared contracting a disease. When visitors came to call, she insisted they come no closer than ten feet.

All her philanthropic activities with the villagers were abandoned. Each afternoon, she would order the car to be brought around. Lying in the rear seat, she would careen madly through the countryside, urging her chauffeur to greater and greater speed.

One autumn afternoon in September 1923, a reporter from an English newspaper came to interview her on her eighty-fifth birthday. They sat in the garden and sipped tea. To her relief, he seemed to know nothing about the colorful past she had tried so hard to live down. His questions dealt with women's rights; in fact, he called her "The United States Mother of Woman's Suffrage."

"What do you think of the current bill to give Englishwomen the vote at twenty-five?" he asked.

Vicky answered obliquely. "I want women to have the vote as soon as they are fit to use it, but I do not believe in forced maturity."

Then she explained that she had become a bride when hardly more than a child, and her youth had been unhappy as a result.

After he'd gone, she sat there for a long time. The sun, red as a ripe strawberry, was just beginning to descend. She gazed at the sky, its canopy streaked with lavender and gold and rose, and allowed waves of memory to wash over her. She thought of herself as a young girl in Ohio when she had eaten too many green apples in the orchard behind their shack. She saw herself on the stage at Steinway Hall when somebody asked if she were a "free lover." "Yes," she had answered proudly, "yes." Ah, how young and tough she had been then! Again she thought of the day, a half century ago, when she had been nominated for the Presidency, could picture that heady spring afternoon with its star-spangled banners and hear the tumultuous voices crying, "Aye, aye." What a monstrous trick life had played on her, tantalizing her with such a magnificent destiny and then holding it beyond her reach.

In the end, when she craved peace of mind, she found herself paralyzed by fear. Ever since Tennie's funeral, she could think of nothing but dying. The realization that her time was drawing closer terrified her. She could smell the scent of fear rising from her pores. And though she pinched her nostrils, the deadly perfume lingered.

She was not ready for death; she hadn't come to terms with life yet.

For the next three years, she refused to go to bed. If she lay down, death might snatch her unawares. Instead, she slept sitting up in a chair.

On June 9, 1927—at the age of eighty-eight—she died in her sleep.

Epilogue

At Victoria Woodhull's death in 1927, times had changed radically in some ways since her struggles in the 1870s; in other ways, they had not changed at all. By 1927, women could vote, work in an office, drink, smoke cigarettes, and shorten their hemlines above their knees. Although they no longer had to pretend they were pure and virginal, they still worried about being thought "fast." Feminism had gone beyond respectability and dullness—it was dead.

Despite the greater opportunities open to women, society's attitude toward them remained essentially the same. The life of the average woman in the 1920s was little different from that of a woman in Vicky's day. Woman's place was supposed to be the home. Her destiny was to marry and become a mother and homemaker. Little girls planned to raise children when they grew up; little boys said they wanted to be President. In fact, most jobs outside the home were still reserved "for men only."

Some historians have claimed that Vicky set feminism back a hundred years. In a sense, this is true. The questions she raised—the issues of sex, marriage, and female revolution—took much of the steam out of the women's movement in the nineteenth century. She caused feminists to retreat to safer ground where they concentrated on getting the vote. They became timid reformers instead of revolutionaries.

Vicky brought up questions so terrifying that generations of women would be afraid to touch them again. Not until the late 1960s would feminists once more begin to pick up where Vicky left off.

* * *

Can a woman be elected President? Victoria Woodhull's question still has not been answered. The American political system has yet to catch up with the ideas that scandalized her generation.

Unsuccessful as Vicky's crusade had been, others took up her dream. Twelve years after she ran for President, attorney Belva Ann Lockwood became the second woman in our history to declare herself a presidential candidate. A fervent feminist, she was, in contrast to Vicky, a restrained fighter for women's rights and a paragon of respectability. Discrimination was familiar to her. As a teacher in Royalton, New York, before the Civil War, she had protested loudly when paid half of what male teachers received.

Later, after graduating from law school, she found herself barred from practicing before the United States Supreme Court. "Women are not needed in the courts," said the judge who denied her petition. "Their place is in the home to wait upon their husbands, to bring up the children, to cook the meals, make beds, polish pans and dust furniture."

Unwilling to trade her law degree for a dustcloth, Belva drafted a bill permitting women to practice before the Supreme Court. It took her three years to get it passed by Congress, but finally, in 1879, she became the first woman to appear before the country's highest tribunal.

In the election year of 1884, feminists tried to persuade both the Democratic and Republican conventions to write a strong women's rights plank into their campaign platforms. Both parties ignored their requests. Insulted women around the country urged Belva, then fifty-four and twice widowed, to run for President.

She was formally nominated as the candidate of the National Equal Rights party. Marietta L. Stow of California was selected as her running mate. The nomination took place in a Maryland apple orchard just outside Washington, D.C. A makeshift platform under the trees was festooned with flags, banners, and pictures of the candidates. Campaign buttons, as well as homemade cakes and pies, were distributed to the delegates.

In many states, giggling young men organized Mother Hubbard Clubs and Broom Brigades. Parading through the streets dressed in women's clothing and carrying brooms and mops, they mockingly chanted, "Elect a lady to the White House." Belva said she found them amusing. Although her campaign attracted nationwide attention, she held no hope of winning. She regarded her candidacy only as a means of publicizing the feminist cause. Writing to a group of supporters in California, she explained: "This campaign will become the entering wedge, the first practical movement in the history of woman suffrage. It will open a door to be shut no more forever."

Despite her impressive background as an attorney, the voters sent Grover Cleveland to the White House. Belva received only 4149 of the more than 10 million votes cast. Her supporters charged that many of her ballots had been thrown out.

Belva failed to be dismayed by her poor showing. She ran again in 1888. "My dear," she later told her daughter Lura, "the fact that a woman actually ran for President will give men something to think about for years to come."

Her prediction turned out to be dead wrong. Not only men, but women as well, promptly forgot that women had run for President in the nineteenth century. In 1964, when Senator Margaret Chase Smith of Maine announced her candidacy, it was mistakenly believed that she was the first female contestant. Senator Smith's campaign created little excitement among the members of either sex. Next to Belva's, it rated staid; compared to Vicky's, it seemed like a Sunday school picnic.

Women won the right to vote in 1920 but made little use of their hard-won franchise. They voted like their menfolk, and on the rare occasions when they ran for political office, it was for seats vacated by their dead husbands. For decades, women remained the gofers of politics. Working behind the scenes, they sealed envelopes, ran mimeograph machines, and made phone calls and coffee.

Not until the 1970s did significant numbers of women

turn their attention to winning public office in no-holds-barred races. They didn't worry about being "ladies"; they campaigned to win. They also found that they could count on strong support from their own sex. The National Women's Political Caucus was formed to inspire women to run for political office. Another nonpartisan group, the Women's National Education Fund, began to conduct regional seminars encouraging women candidates and offering instruction on campaign tactics.

Despite these promising signs, women still faced enormous obstacles rooted in culture and tradition. In 1972 Shirley Chisholm, congresswoman from Brooklyn, made a fierce stab at the Democratic nomination for President. She was unsuccessful.

In 1974 more than fifteen hundred women—the largest number ever—battled their way through the primaries. When the election results were tallied, they showed that women had scored significant gains at all levels of government, and a few had even been elected to offices that women had never held before. For example, Ella Grasso of Connecticut became the first woman governor to be chosen in her own right instead of as a replacement for her husband. Janet Gray Hayes was elected mayor of San Jose, California, the first woman to govern a city of more than a half million population. And Susie Sharp of North Carolina became the first woman chief justice of a state supreme court.

The woman who started it all has never been awarded her rightful place in America's political history. Victoria Woodhull's candidacy has not been considered sufficiently important to include in school textbooks. No monuments nor commemorative stamps have memorialized her. In Homer, Ohio, no marker notes her birthplace. As recently as 1957, however, at least one person in Homer remembered her. A reporter from the Cleveland *Plain-Dealer* talked to Frank Yoakam, an eighty-nine-year-old retired storekeeper, who recalled meeting Vicky when he was a boy.

On one of Vicky's trips back to America in the 1880s, she paid a last, brief visit to Homer. Yoakam said he talked to her for ten minutes, an event he apparently never forgot. His memory seemed to be excellent. He recalled that she arrived in a stylish carriage with a fringe. He also gave a detailed description of her outfit: a brown silk dress, a hat with ostrich feathers, and a diamond, heart-shaped locket that hung from a string of pearls around her neck.

"She was the most beautiful woman I had ever seen," he sighed. "I can see how she won all the men she did."

What he failed to remember was that she had ever run for President.

Perhaps the most perceptive assessment of Vicky's contribution to women's liberation was made before she was erased and forgotten by history. In 1875, Elizabeth Cady Stanton wrote:

Victoria Woodhull has done a work for women that none of us could have done. She has faced and dared men to call her the names that make women shudder. She has risked and realized the sort of ignominy that would have paralyzed any of us . . . Leaping into the brambles that were too high for us to see over them, she broke a path into their close and thorny intersticces, with a steadfast faith that glorious principle would triumph at last over conspicuous ignominy, although her life might be sacrificed. And when with a meteor's dash, she sank into a dismal swamp, we could not lift her out of the mire nor buoy her through the deadly waters. She will be as famous as she has been infamous, made so by benighted or cowardly men and women. In the annals of emancipation, the name of Victoria Woodhull will have its own high place as a deliverer.

Bibliography

Amundsen, Kirsten. *The Silenced Majority.* Englewood Cliffs, N.J.: Prentice-Hall, 1971.

Chafe, William H. *The American Woman.* New York: Oxford University Press, 1972.

Crow, Duncan. *The Victorian Woman.* New York: Stein & Day, 1972.

Flexner, Eleanor. *Century of Struggle.* New York: Atheneum, 1968.

Hale, William H. *Horace Greeley: Voice of the People.* New York: Harper & Bros., 1950.

Johnston, Johanna. *Mrs. Satan. The Incredible Saga of Victoria C. Woodhull.* New York: G.P. Putnam's Sons, 1967.

Kisner, Arlene. *Woodhull and Claflin's Weekly. The Lives and Writings of Notorious Victoria Woodhull and Her Sister Tennessee Claflin.* Washington, N.J.: Times Change Press, 1972.

Lens, Sidney. *Radicalism in America.* New York: Thomas Y. Crowell, 1966.

Nevins, Allan. *The Emergence of Modern America, 1865-1878.* New York: Macmillan, 1927.

O'Neill, William L. *Everyone Was Brave.* Chicago: Quadrangle Books, 1969.

Riegel, Robert E. *American Women.* Cranbury, N.J.: Associated University Presses, 1970.

Ross, Ishbel. *Charmers and Cranks*. New York: Harper & Row, 1965.

___. *Sons of Adam, Daughters of Eve*. New York: Harper & Row, 1969.

Rugoff, Milton. *Prudery and Passion*. New York: G. P. Putnam's Sons, 1971.

Sachs, Emanie. *The Terrible Siren*. New York: Harper & Bros., 1928.

Schneir, Miriam, ed. *Feminism: The Essential Historical Writings*. New York: Random House, 1972.

Seitz, Don C. *The "Also Rans."* Freeport, N.Y.: Books for Libraries Press, 1928.

Shaplen, Robert. *Free Love and Heavenly Sinners, The Story of the Great Henry Ward Beecher Scandal*. New York: Alfred A. Knopf, 1954.

Smith, Page. *Daughters of the Promised Land*. Boston: Little, Brown, 1970.

Sochem, June. *Movers and Shakers*. New York: Quadrangle/New York Times Books, 1973.

Tilton, Theodore. *Victoria C. Woodlmll. A Biographical Sketch*. New York: Golden Age Tract No. 3, 1871.

Woodhull, Victoria C, and Claflin, Tennie C, eds. *Woodhull and Claflin's Weekly*, vols. 1-12 (May 14, 1870-June 10, 1876).

About the Author

Marion Meade studied at Northwestern University in Illinois and later received a master's from Columbia Graduate School of Journalism. She worked as a freelance writer and her articles have appeared in leading magazines and newspapers, including the *New York Times, McCall's,* the *Village Voice, Ms. Magazine,* and *Cosmopolitan.* Meade has written novels, biographies, and nonfiction books. *Bitching* was a significant contribution to the second phase of development in the feminist movement. She has written biographies of Victoria Woodhull (*Free Woman*), Eleanor of Aquitaine, Madame Blavatsky, Buster Keaton (*Cut to the Chase*), Woody Allen (*The Unruly Life of Woody Allen*), and Dorothy Parker (*What Fresh Hell Is This?*). She has published two historical novels: *Sybille,* which narrates the life of a woman troubadour in thirteenth century southern France, during Europe's first great holocaust, the Albigensian crusade; and *Stealing Heaven, The Love Story of Heloise and Abelard.* She lives in New York City.

OPEN **❶** ROAD
INTEGRATED MEDIA

Open Road Integrated Media is a digital publisher and multimedia content company. Open Road creates connections between authors and their audiences by marketing its ebooks through a new proprietary online platform, which uses premium video content and social media.